Low Cholesterol
Cookbook for Beginners UK

1600 Days of Delicious and Balanced Recipes with 30 Days Meal Plan to Enhance Cardiovascular Function and Reduce Cholesterol Levels

Summer Bowen

CONTENTS

Introduction

As an experienced dietician and nutritionist, I have had the privilege of helping many people manage their cholesterol levels through dietary changes. However, I have noticed that there is a lack of accessible and easy-to-follow resources for people who are just starting their journey towards a low-cholesterol diet. That's why I decided to write the Low Cholesterol Cookbook for Beginners UK: 1600 Days of Delicious and Balanced Recipes with 30 Days Meal Plan to Enhance Cardiovascular Function and Reduce Cholesterol Levels.

This cookbook is designed to be a comprehensive and user-friendly resource for anyone looking to improve their cholesterol levels through dietary changes. It includes over 1600 days of delicious and balanced recipes, as well as a 30-day meal plan to help individuals get started on their journey towards better heart health.

The recipes in this cookbook are specifically designed to help enhance cardiovascular function and reduce cholesterol levels. They are packed with nutrient-dense ingredients that are low in cholesterol and saturated fats, making them perfect for individuals looking to make healthier food choices. The diverse recipe options include breakfast, lunch, dinner, and snack ideas, ensuring that there is something for everyone.

One of the key benefits of this cookbook is its emphasis on balance. While it is important to reduce cholesterol intake, it is equally important to make sure that your body is getting all the nutrients it needs to function properly. That's why the recipes in this cookbook are designed to be both delicious and balanced, ensuring that individuals can enjoy healthy meals without feeling deprived.

Another benefit of this cookbook is that the recipes are easy to follow and include simple instructions and ingredient lists. This makes it easy for beginners and experienced cooks alike to create healthy, delicious meals. The recipes are also designed to be balanced, ensuring that individuals are getting all the essential nutrients they need to support their overall health and wellbeing.

The Low Cholesterol Cookbook for Beginners UK is a highly valuable resource for individuals seeking to improve their heart health through dietary changes. With its diverse recipe collection, easy-to-follow instructions, and comprehensive meal plan, this cookbook offers something for everyone, regardless of their skill level or dietary preferences. By incorporating the delicious and balanced recipes from this cookbook into your diet, you can take control of your cholesterol levels and support your overall heart health.

What is low cholesterol and why is it important for heart health?

Cholesterol is a waxy substance found in the body that is necessary for cell growth and hormone production. However, high levels of cholesterol in the blood can increase the risk of heart disease. Low cholesterol refers to maintaining healthy levels of cholesterol in the blood through diet and lifestyle changes. By reducing the amount of saturated and trans fats in the diet, and increasing the intake of fiber-rich foods, it is possible to lower cholesterol levels. This is important for heart health because high cholesterol can lead to the buildup of plaque in the arteries, which can increase the risk of heart attack and stroke. By maintaining healthy cholesterol levels, individuals can reduce their risk of heart disease and improve overall cardiovascular health.

How can the Low Cholesterol Cookbook help me manage my cholesterol levels?

The Low Cholesterol Cookbook is a valuable resource for individuals looking to manage their cholesterol levels through diet. The cookbook offers a variety of recipes that are low in saturated and trans fats and high in fiber, which can help reduce cholesterol levels in the blood. Here are some ways in which the Low Cholesterol Cookbook can help manage cholesterol levels:

- **Reducing Saturated and Trans Fats**

The recipes in the Low Cholesterol Cookbook are designed to be low in saturated and trans fats. These fats can raise LDL (bad) cholesterol levels in the blood, which can increase the risk of heart disease. By reducing the amount of these fats in the diet, individuals can help manage their cholesterol levels and reduce their risk of heart disease.

- **Increasing Fiber Intake**

The Low Cholesterol Cookbook emphasizes the importance of fiber-rich foods in the diet. Fiber can help lower cholesterol levels in the blood by binding to cholesterol and removing it from the body. By increasing the amount of fiber in the diet through recipes that include whole grains, fruits, and vegetables, individuals can help manage their cholesterol levels.

- **Providing Nutritional Information**

Each recipe in the Low Cholesterol Cookbook includes nutritional information, including the amount of cholesterol, saturated fat, and trans fat. This information can help individuals make informed decisions about what they eat and how it may impact their cholesterol levels.

- **Offering Variety**

The Low Cholesterol Cookbook offers a wide variety of recipes, including breakfast, lunch, dinner, and snack options. This variety can help individuals maintain a healthy diet while managing their cholesterol levels and avoiding boredom with their meals.

- **Providing Guidance on Healthy Eating**

In addition to offering recipes, the Low Cholesterol Cookbook provides guidance on healthy eating habits. This includes tips on portion control, meal planning, and healthy cooking techniques. By adopting these healthy habits, individuals can help manage their cholesterol levels and improve their overall health.

- **Encouraging Lifestyle Changes**

The Low Cholesterol Cookbook is not just a cookbook, but also a guide to making lifestyle changes to support heart health. By adopting healthy eating habits and incorporating regular exercise into their routine, individuals can help manage their cholesterol levels and reduce their risk of heart disease.

What are some benefits of a low-cholesterol diet?

A low-cholesterol diet is beneficial for overall health, and can help reduce the risk of heart disease, stroke, and other health conditions. Here are some of the key benefits of a low-cholesterol diet:

- **Reduced risk of heart disease**

High cholesterol levels in the blood can lead to the buildup of plaque in the arteries, which can increase the risk of heart disease. A low-cholesterol diet can help lower cholesterol levels in the blood, reducing the risk of heart disease and related conditions.

- **Improved cardiovascular health**

In addition to lowering cholesterol levels, a low-cholesterol diet can improve overall cardiovascular health. By focusing on nutrient-dense foods such as fruits, vegetables, whole grains, and lean proteins, individuals can support their heart health and reduce the risk of other cardiovascular conditions.

- **Weight management**

Many high-cholesterol foods are also high in calories and fat, which can contribute to weight gain. By reducing the amount of these foods in the diet, individuals can manage their weight and support overall health.

- **Improved digestion**

A low-cholesterol diet often emphasizes foods that are high in fiber, such as fruits, vegetables, and whole grains. These foods can help improve digestion and promote regular bowel movements.

- **Reduced inflammation**

A diet high in saturated and trans fats can contribute to inflammation in the body, which can increase the risk of chronic disease. By reducing the amount of these fats in the diet, individuals can help reduce inflammation and support overall health.

- **Improved energy levels**

A diet high in processed and high-fat foods can contribute to feelings of sluggishness and fatigue. By adopting a low-cholesterol diet rich in nutrient-dense foods, individuals can improve their energy levels and feel more alert and focused throughout the day.

- **Reduced risk of other health conditions**

In addition to heart disease and stroke, high cholesterol levels in the blood can increase the risk of other health conditions such as type 2 diabetes and certain cancers. By managing cholesterol levels through diet, individuals can reduce their risk of these conditions as well.

What types of ingredients are included in the Low Cholesterol Cookbook?

- **Fruits and Vegetables**

The Low Cholesterol Cookbook features a variety of fruits and vegetables, including leafy greens, berries, citrus fruits, cruciferous vegetables, and more. These foods are high in fiber, vitamins, minerals, and other nutrients that support overall health.

- **Whole Grains**

Whole grains are an important part of the Low Cholesterol Cookbook's recipes. These include foods such as brown rice, quinoa, oats, and whole wheat bread. Whole grains are high in fiber and provide sustained energy throughout the day.

- **Lean Proteins**

The cookbook features lean proteins such as chicken, turkey, fish, and plant-based proteins such as lentils, beans, and tofu. These proteins are low in saturated fat and provide essential amino acids for building and repairing tissues.

- **Nuts and Seeds**

Nuts and seeds are a great source of healthy fats, protein, and fiber. The cookbook includes a variety of nuts and seeds, including almonds, walnuts, chia seeds, and flax seeds.

- **Healthy Fats**

The Low Cholesterol Cookbook includes healthy fats such as olive oil, avocado, and coconut oil. These fats are rich in monounsaturated and polyunsaturated fats, which can help lower cholesterol levels in the blood.

- **Herbs and Spices**

The cookbook emphasizes the use of herbs and spices to add flavor to meals without adding salt or unhealthy fats. Common herbs and spices used in the cookbook include garlic, ginger, basil, oregano, and turmeric.

Breakfast And Brunch

Cantaloupe And Cauliflower Smoothies

Servings: X
Cooking Time: X
Ingredients:

- 2 cups vanilla soy milk
- ½ cantaloupe, cut into chunks
- ½ cup nonfat vanilla Greek yogurt
- ½ cup cooked mashed cauliflower
- 2 tablespoons honey
- ¼ teaspoon ground cinnamon

Directions:

1. In a blender, add the milk, cantaloupe, yogurt, cauliflower, honey, and cinnamon and process until smooth.
2. Pour into glasses and serve immediately.

Nutrition Info:

- Info Per Serving: Calories: 183 ; Fat:1 g ;Saturated fat: 0 g ;Sodium: 112 mg

Cinnamon-hazelnut Scones

Servings: 8
Cooking Time: X
Ingredients:

- 1 cup all-purpose flour
- 1 cup whole-wheat flour
- 1/3 cup brown sugar
- 1 teaspoon cinnamon
- 1 teaspoon baking powder
- ½ teaspoon baking soda
- 3 tablespoons butter or plant sterol margarine
- 3 tablespoons canola oil
- 1 egg
- ½ cup buttermilk
- 1 teaspoon vanilla
- ½ cup dried cranberries
- ½ cup chopped hazelnuts
- 1 tablespoon milk

Directions:

1. Preheat oven to 400ºF. Line cookie sheet with parchment paper and set aside. In large bowl, combine flour, whole-wheat flour, brown sugar, cinnamon, baking powder, and baking soda and mix well. Cut in butter until particles are fine.
2. In small bowl, combine oil, egg, buttermilk, and vanilla and beat to combine. Add to dry ingredients and mix just until moistened.
3. Add cranberries and hazelnuts and mix just until blended. Turn out onto floured surface and toss several times to coat.
4. Pat dough into an 8″ circle on prepared cookie sheet. Cut into 8 triangles and separate slightly. Brush with milk. Bake for 15 to 18 minutes or until scones are golden brown. Cool for 5 minutes, then serve.

Nutrition Info:

- Info Per Serving: Calories:286.34 ; Fat:14.98 g ;Saturated fat:3.77 g ;Sodium:184.16 mg

Basil-tomato Pizza

Servings: 6
Cooking Time: X
Ingredients:

- 1 tablespoon olive oil
- 3 cloves garlic, minced
- 4 tomatoes
- ½ teaspoon dried oregano leaves
- 1/8 teaspoon white pepper
- ½ cup torn fresh basil leaves
- 1 Whole-Grain Pizza Crust , prebaked
- 1 cup shredded provolone cheese

Directions:

1. Preheat oven to 400ºF. In small saucepan, heat olive oil over medium heat. Add garlic; cook for 2–3 minutes or until garlic is fragrant. Remove from heat and set aside.
2. Cut tomatoes in half and gently squeeze out seeds. Chop tomatoes and combine with oregano, pepper, and basil leaves in small bowl.
3. Place crust on cookie sheet or pizza stone. Brush with the garlic mixture. Top with tomato mixture, then sprinkle with cheese. Bake for 15–20 minutes or until pizza is hot and cheese melts and bubbles. Serve immediately.

Nutrition Info:

- Info Per Serving: Calories: 334.64 ; Fat: 11.54 g ;Saturated fat: 4.59g ;Sodium: 303.68 mg

Tofu And Cucumber Spring Rolls

Servings: 5
Cooking Time: 20 Minutes
Ingredients:

- ⅓ cup Tangy Soy Sauce
- 3 tablespoons nut butter (almond, cashew, or all-natural peanut butter)
- 6 ounces firm tofu, cut into 10 (½-inch wide) strips
- 5 rehydrated rice paper wraps
- 1 cucumber, peeled and cut into sticks

Directions:

1. Preheat the oven to 425°F. Line a baking sheet with parchment paper and set aside.
2. In a small bowl, mix the Tangy Soy Sauce and the nut butter until well blended.
3. Drizzle 2 to 3 tablespoons of the sauce mixture over the tofu strips. You'll have some sauce left over. You can use this for dipping.
4. Place the tofu strips on the prepared baking sheet and bake for 20 minutes.
5. Place the rehydrated rice paper wraps on a flat surface.
6. Once the tofu is done cooking, place two strips of tofu and a few cucumber sticks in the center of one wrap.
7. Fold the sides of the rice paper over the filling, then tightly roll from the bottom up all the way until the wrap is sealed. Repeat with the other wraps.
8. Enjoy the spring rolls with the dipping sauce.

Nutrition Info:

- Info Per Serving: Calories:181 ; Fat: 8g ;Saturated fat: 1g ;Sodium: 255mg

Lean Beef Lettuce Wraps

Servings: 5
Cooking Time: 15 Minutes
Ingredients:

- 1 pound lean ground beef
- ½ white onion, diced
- ⅓ cup Honey-Garlic Sauce
- 1 tablespoon white vinegar
- 10 large lettuce leaves, washed and dried

Directions:

1. In a large skillet over high heat, cook the ground beef for 10 minutes until browned. Drain the fat.
2. Add the onion, Honey-Garlic Sauce, and vinegar to the pan, and cook an additional 3 to 5 minutes. Evenly divide the beef mixture between the lettuce leaves and fold them over. Enjoy immediately.

Nutrition Info:

- Info Per Serving: Calories:172 ; Fat: 7g ;Saturated fat:2g ;Sodium: 577mg;

Rolled Oats Cereal

Servings: 4
Cooking Time: 5 Min
Ingredients:

- 2 tbsp. plant-based butter, plus 1 tablespoon unsalted butter
- 1 tbsp. organic honey
- ¾ cup rolled oats
- ⅓ cup walnuts, roughly chopped
- 1 tbsp. chia seeds
- 1 tbsp. hemp seeds
- 1 tbsp. ground flaxseed
- ½ tsp ground cinnamon
- Pinch fine sea salt
- 2 tbsp. dried cranberries
- 2 tbsp. raisins

Directions:

1. In a large heavy bottom pan, melt the butter and honey over medium heat, cook until bubbly.
2. Mix in the oats, walnuts, chia seeds, hemp seeds, flaxseed, cinnamon, and salt. Cook for 3 to 4 minutes, stirring until the oats and nuts start to brown. If the mixture is browning too fast, turn the heat down to low. Remove from the heat and add the cranberries and raisins, mix to combine.
3. Eat the oat cereal right away or cool it completely, then store it in an airtight container.

Nutrition Info:

- Info Per Serving: Calories: 230 ; Fat: 16 g ;Saturated fat: 3 g ;Sodium: 64 mg

Cranberry Orange Mixed Grain Granola

Servings: 6
Cooking Time: 20 Minutes
Ingredients:

- 1 cup regular rolled oats
- ½ cup barley flakes
- 1 cup kamut flakes or corn or wheat flakes
- ⅓ cup sunflower seeds
- 3 tablespoons pure maple syrup
- 1 tablespoon safflower oil
- 1 tablespoon orange juice
- 1 teaspoon vanilla extract
- 2 teaspoons fresh orange zest
- ½ cup chopped dried cranberries

Directions:

1. Preheat the oven to 350°F.
2. In a large bowl, combine the rolled oats, barley flakes, kamut flakes, and sunflower seeds.
3. In a small bowl, combine the maple syrup, safflower oil, orange juice, vanilla, and orange zest, mixing well.
4. Drizzle the maple syrup mixture over the grains and toss to coat.
5. Spread the mixture in a baking sheet.
6. Bake for 15 to 20 minutes, stirring once, until the mixture is lightly toasted.
7. Stir in the cranberries, let the granola cool completely, and store in an airtight container at room temperature for up to 1 week.

Nutrition Info:

- Info Per Serving: Calories: 226 ; Fat: 8 g ;Saturated fat: 1 g ;Sodium: 47 mg

Cranberry-orange Bread

Servings: 12
Cooking Time: X
Ingredients:
- ¼ cup orange juice
- 2 tablespoons frozen orange juice concentrate, thawed
- ½ teaspoon almond extract
- ¼ cup canola oil
- 1 egg
- 1/3 cup sugar
- ½ cup brown sugar
- 1 teaspoon grated orange zest
- 1½ cups all-purpose flour
- ¼ cup whole-wheat flour
- 1 teaspoon baking soda
- 1 teaspoon baking powder
- 2 cups chopped cranberries
- ½ cup chopped hazelnuts

Directions:
1. Preheat oven to 350ºF. Spray a 9″ × 5″ loaf pan with nonstick cooking spray containing flour, and set aside.
2. In medium bowl, combine orange juice, orange juice concentrate, almond extract, canola oil, egg, sugar, brown sugar, and orange zest and beat to combine.
3. In large bowl, combine flour, whole-wheat flour, baking soda, baking powder, and mix. Make a well in the center of the flour mixture and pour in the orange juice mixture. Stir just until dry ingredients are moistened.
4. Fold in cranberries and hazelnuts. Pour into prepared pan. Bake for 55–65 minutes or until bread is golden-brown and toothpick inserted in center comes out clean. Remove from pan and let cool on wire rack.

Nutrition Info:
- Info Per Serving: Calories: 232.48; Fat: 8.24 g ;Saturated fat:0.72g ;Sodium: 145.81 mg

Creamed Rice

Servings: 2
Cooking Time: 20 Min
Ingredients:
- ½ cup brown basmati rice
- 2 cups water
- 1 cup unsweetened almond milk, plus extra for serving
- 1 tsp vanilla extract
- ⅛ tsp ground cinnamon
- Pinch fine sea salt
- ¼ cup dried raisins
- ¼ cup unsalted mixed nuts, chopped
- 2 tbsp. organic honey

Directions:
1. Place the basmati rice in a large-sized mixing bowl and add the water. Soak overnight in the refrigerator, then drain.
2. Add the soaked rice, water, almond milk, vanilla extract, cinnamon, and fine sea salt in a medium-sized stockpot and place over medium heat.
3. Bring the rice mixture to a boil and then reduce the heat to low. Simmer for 20 minutes, until the rice is tender and most of the liquid has been absorbed, stirring frequently.
4. Remove the stockpot from the heat and mix in the raisins, nuts, and honey. Add extra almond milk if you prefer a thinner pudding.
5. Serve.

Nutrition Info:
- Info Per Serving: Calories: 341; Fat: 8g ;Saturated fat: 0g ;Sodium: 213mg

Steel-cut Oatmeal With Dried Apples And Pecans

Servings: X
Cooking Time: 10 Minutes
Ingredients:

- 1 cup quick-cooking steel-cut oats
- 1½ cups unsweetened soy milk
- 1 cup water
- 2 tablespoons maple syrup
- 1 small apple, cored and chopped
- ¼ teaspoon ground cinnamon
- 2 tablespoons chopped pecans, for garnish

Directions:

1. Add the oats, soy milk, water, maple syrup, apple, and cinnamon to a medium saucepan, stirring to combine.
2. Place the pan over medium-high heat and cook the mixture, stirring frequently, until the oats start to simmer.
3. Reduce the heat to low and continue cooking, stirring frequently, until the oats are tender, about 5 minutes.
4. Serve the oatmeal warm, topped with the pecans.

Nutrition Info:

- Info Per Serving: Calories: 330; Fat: 8g ;Saturated fat: 1g ;Sodium: 104 mg

Savory Breakfast Rice Porridge

Servings: 5
Cooking Time: 1 Hour 5 Minutes
Ingredients:

- 1 pound firm tofu, drained and sliced into 1-inch cubes
- 2 tablespoons low-sodium soy sauce
- 1 tablespoon minced garlic
- 9 cups water
- 1 cup rinsed uncooked brown rice
- 1 cup chopped spinach
- Sea salt
- Freshly ground black pepper

Directions:

1. In a medium bowl, place the tofu, soy sauce, and garlic. Let marinate in the refrigerator for 30 minutes.
2. While the tofu is marinating, in a large saucepan, combine the water and brown rice and bring to a boil over high heat, then reduce the heat to medium-high and simmer for 60 minutes, whisking occasionally.
3. Whisk the cooked rice porridge to your desired consistency.
4. Add the tofu and the marinade to the porridge and bring it to a boil, then simmer for 2 to 3 minutes, until fragrant.
5. Stir in the spinach and season with salt and pepper. Serve warm.

Nutrition Info:

- Info Per Serving: Calories: 276 ; Fat: 9g ;Saturated fat: 1 g ;Sodium: 255mg

Cranberry Hotcakes

Servings: 2
Cooking Time: 9 Min
Ingredients:

- 1 cup rolled oats
- 1 cup cranberries
- 3 tbsp. fat-free plain yoghurt
- ¼ cup unsweetened almond milk
- 1 tbsp. ground flaxseed
- 1 large egg
- ½ tsp ground cinnamon
- 2 tsp avocado oil

Directions:

1. In a medium-sized mixing bowl, mix the oats, cranberries, yoghurt, almond milk, flax seeds, egg, and cinnamon together, until it becomes a thick batter.
2. In a large nonstick frying pan, heat the avocado oil over medium-low heat. Pour ¼ cup of the batter into the pan and fry for 2 to 3 minutes, or until bubbles start to form on top, flip, and fry for 2 minutes, or until lightly browned and fully cooked. Continue with the remaining batter.
3. Serve with your favorite toppings.

Nutrition Info:

- Info Per Serving: Calories: 328 ; Fat: 12g ;Saturated fat: 2 g ;Sodium: 54 mg

Panzanella Breakfast Casserole

Servings: X
Cooking Time: 35 Minutes
Ingredients:

- Nonstick olive oil cooking spray
- 1 teaspoon olive oil
- ¼ cup chopped sweet onion
- 1 teaspoon minced garlic
- 2 slices multigrain bread, cut into ½-inch chunks
- ¼ cup chopped artichoke hearts
- ¼ cup sliced black olives
- ¼ cup sliced sun-dried tomatoes
- 12 ounces firm tofu, drained and pressed (see tip, Chili-Sautéed Tofu with Almonds)
- ½ cup soy milk
- ½ teaspoon chopped fresh basil

Directions:

1. Preheat the oven to 350°F. Lightly spray 2 (8-ounce) ramekins with cooking spray and set aside.
2. Warm the olive oil in a small skillet over medium-high heat.
3. Add the onion and garlic and sauté until translucent, about 3 minutes.
4. Transfer the onion mixture to a medium bowl and stir in the bread, artichoke hearts, olives, and sun-dried tomatoes, tossing well to mix.
5. In a blender, add the tofu and soy milk and blend until smooth.
6. Add the tofu mixture to the bowl with the bread, add the basil, and stir to combine.
7. Evenly divide the mixture between the ramekins, shaking them to evenly disperse the mixture.
8. Place the ramekins on a baking sheet and bake until the casseroles are set and golden brown, 25 to 30 minutes.
9. Serve.

Nutrition Info:

- Info Per Serving: Calories: 294 ; Fat: 13 g ;Saturated fat: 2 g ;Sodium: 147 mg

Raisin Breakfast Cookies

Servings: 16
Cooking Time: 20 Minutes
Ingredients:
- Olive oil
- 2 bananas
- 3 tablespoons nut butter (such as almond, cashew, or all-natural peanut butter)
- 1 cup steel-cut oats
- ¼ cup raisins
- ¼ cup crushed almonds

Directions:
1. Preheat the oven to 350°F. Lightly grease a baking sheet with olive oil.
2. In a medium bowl, mash the bananas together with nut butter using a fork.
3. Add the oats, raisins, and almonds to the mixture.
4. Roll the dough into 16 balls, about 1 tablespoon each.
5. Place the cookies on the prepared baking sheet and bake for 20 minutes, until they are slightly brown.
6. Let the cookies cool for 10 minutes and serve.

Nutrition Info:
- Info Per Serving: Calories: 89 ; Fat: 4g ;Saturated fat: 0g ;Sodium: 1 mg

Dutch Apple Omelet

Servings: 4
Cooking Time: X
Ingredients:
- 2 Granny Smith apples, thinly sliced
- ¼ cup water
- 1 tablespoon butter or margarine
- 1 tablespoon brown sugar
- ½ teaspoon cinnamon
- ½ cup egg substitute
- 4 large egg whites
- ¼ cup skim milk
- ½ cup Cinnamon Granola (page 24)

Directions:
1. In large nonstick skillet, combine apple slices and water. Bring to a boil over high heat, reduce heat to low, and simmer for 4–5 minutes or until apples are almost tender.
2. Drain the water and add butter, brown sugar, and cinnamon to apples; cook and stir over medium heat for 1 minute. Arrange apples in even layer in skillet.
3. In large bowl, combine egg substitute, egg whites, and milk and beat with eggbeater or wire whisk. Pour into skillet and cook over medium heat, shaking pan and lifting edges of omelet occasionally, until browned on the bottom and set but still moist on top. Sprinkle with Cinnamon Granola, flip in half, slide onto serving plate, and serve immediately.

Nutrition Info:
- Info Per Serving: Calories: 237.84; Fat: 9.78 g ;Saturated fat:4.14 g ;Sodium: 180.82 mg

French Toast With Citrus Compote

Servings: 4–6
Cooking Time: X
Ingredients:
- 1 orange
- 1 red grapefruit
- ½ cup sugar, divided
- 1 cup orange juice, divided
- 1 teaspoon vanilla
- 1 egg
- 6 slices Hearty-Grain French Bread
- 2 tablespoons butter or margarine

Directions:
1. Peel and chop orange and grapefruit and place in small bowl. In small saucepan, combine ¼ cup sugar with ½ cup orange juice and bring to a simmer. Simmer for 5–6 minutes or until slightly thickened; pour over orange mixture and set aside.
2. In shallow bowl, combine remaining ¼ cup sugar with ½ cup orange juice, vanilla, and egg, and beat well. Heat a nonstick pan over medium heat and add butter.
3. Slice bread on an angle. Dip bread into egg mixture, turning to coat. Cook in hot butter over medium heat for 6–8 minutes, turning once, until bread is crisp and deep golden brown. Serve with citrus compote.

Nutrition Info:
- Info Per Serving: Calories:262.24 ; Fat:4.59 g ;Saturated fat:2.07 g ;Sodium: 96.68 mg

Fish Tacos

Servings: 5
Cooking Time: 20 Minutes
Ingredients:
- 1 pound white fish (such as tilapia), cut into bite-size pieces
- 1 tablespoon olive oil
- Sea salt
- Freshly ground black pepper
- 1 cup low-fat plain Greek yogurt
- 5 (6½-inch) whole wheat or whole-grain corn tortillas
- 2½ cups shredded romaine lettuce
- 2 tablespoons freshly squeezed lime juice

Directions:
1. In a medium bowl, mix the salmon, Spicy Honey Sauce, and Preheat the oven to 375°F. Line a baking sheet with parchment paper.
2. Season the fish with the olive oil, salt, and pepper. Place the fish on the prepared baking sheet and bake for 20 minutes, until slightly golden brown.
3. While the fish is cooking, in a small bowl, combine the yogurt with another pinch of salt and pepper.
4. Once the fish is cooked, place ⅕ of the fish in a tortilla with ½ cup romaine, 1 teaspoon lime juice, and a dollop of yogurt. Repeat with the remaining tortillas and serve immediately.

Nutrition Info:
- Info Per Serving: Calories: 272; Fat: 7g ;Saturated fat: 2g ;Sodium: 450mg

Strawberry Granola Parfaits

Servings: 6
Cooking Time: X
Ingredients:

- 2 (6-ounce) containers strawberry yogurt
- ¼ cup frozen nonfat whipped topping, thawed
- 1½ cups chopped strawberries
- ½ cup raspberries
- 1½ cups Cinnamon Granola
- 2 tablespoons toasted coconut

Directions:
1. In small bowl, combine yogurt with whipped topping; fold together until blended.
2. In six parfait glasses, layer yogurt mixture, granola, and strawberries until glasses are full. Top with raspberries and sprinkle with coconut. Serve immediately, or cover and refrigerate for up to 2 hours before serving. (Granola will soften slightly.)

Nutrition Info:
- Info Per Serving: Calories: 342.21 ; Fat:9.95 g ;Saturated fat: 2.58 g;Sodium: 96.40 mg

Strawberry Yogurt Tarts

Servings: 5
Cooking Time: 2 Hours
Ingredients:

- ½ cup pitted Medjool dates
- ½ cup crushed almonds
- 1 tablespoon maple syrup
- 1 cup low-fat plain Greek yogurt
- ½ cup strawberries
- 2 tablespoons water

Directions:
1. Line 5 cups of a muffin tin with paper liners and set aside.
2. In a food processor or blender, place the dates and pulse for 10 to 20 seconds until they become a paste.
3. Add the crushed almonds and maple syrup to the blender and pulse to mix.
4. Evenly divide the date mixture into the lined cups and press it down firmly; it should fill about one-third of the cup.
5. In a clean blender, blend the yogurt, strawberries, and water until smooth.
6. Pour the fruit and yogurt mixture into the cups until each one is full.
7. Place the cups in the freezer for 2 hours to set, and serve.

Nutrition Info:
- Info Per Serving: Calories: 141; Fat:5g ;Saturated fat:1g ;Sodium: 35mg

Curried Farro Hot Cereal

Servings: 4
Cooking Time: 25 Minutes
Ingredients:

- 1 cup farro
- ½ cup unsweetened apple juice
- 1½ cups water
- ½ cup low-fat soy milk
- 1 tablespoon pure maple syrup, plus more for serving (optional)
- 1 to 2 teaspoons curry powder
- Pinch salt
- ⅓ cup dried currants

Directions:
1. In a medium heavy saucepan, combine the farro, apple juice, water, soy milk, maple syrup, curry powder, and salt. Bring to a simmer over medium heat, then reduce the heat to low.
2. Cover the pot and cook the farro mixture, stirring occasionally, for about 20 minutes. Stir in the currants and cook 5 to 7 minutes longer or until the grains are tender but still chewy.
3. Serve with fresh fruit and a drizzle of maple syrup, if desired.

Nutrition Info:
- Info Per Serving: Calories: 182 ; Fat: 2 g ;Saturated fat: 0 g ;Sodium: 15 mg

Dark-chocolate Orange Scones

Servings: 10
Cooking Time: X
Ingredients:

- 1¼ cups all-purpose flour
- 1 cup whole-wheat flour
- 1/3 cup brown sugar
- ¼ cup cocoa powder
- 1/8 teaspoon salt
- 1 teaspoon baking powder
- ½ teaspoon baking soda
- 5 tablespoons butter or plant sterol margarine
- 1 egg white
- ¼ cup orange juice
- ½ cup buttermilk
- 1 teaspoon vanilla
- 1 teaspoon grated orange zest
- 1 cup dark chocolate chips
- 2 tablespoons sanding sugar

Directions:

1. Preheat oven to 375ºF. Line a cookie sheet with parchment paper and set aside.
2. In large bowl, combine flour, whole-wheat flour, brown sugar, cocoa, salt, baking powder, and baking soda and mix well. Cut in the butter until particles are fine.
3. In small bowl, combine egg white, orange juice, buttermilk, vanilla, and orange zest and mix well. Pour over dry ingredients and stir until moistened. Fold in chocolate chips.
4. Gather dough into a ball and pat into a 9″ circle on the prepared cookie sheet. Cut into 10 wedges and separate slightly. Sprinkle with sanding sugar. Bake for 20–25 minutes or until scones are set.

Nutrition Info:

- Info Per Serving: Calories: 271.10; Fat:11.59 g ;Saturated fat:6.93 g;Sodium: 193.64 mg

Crisp Polenta Open-faced Sandwiches

Servings: 8-10
Cooking Time: X
Ingredients:

- 1 recipe Cheese Polenta
- 1 cup shredded Gruyère cheese
- ¼ cup chopped fresh basil leaves
- 3 tomatoes, sliced
- 7 tablespoons grated Parmesan cheese

Directions:

1. Prepare polenta as directed, except when done, pour onto a greased cookie sheet; spread to a ½″ thick rectangle, about 9″ × 15″. Cover and chill until very firm, about 2 hours.
2. Preheat broiler. Cut polenta into fifteen 3″ squares. Place on broiler pan; broil for 4–6 minutes or until golden brown. Carefully turn polenta and broil for 3–5 minutes or until golden brown.
3. Remove from oven and sprinkle with Gruyère and basil. Top each with a slice of tomato, then Parmesan. Return to broiler and broil for 3–6 minutes or until cheese melts and sandwiches are hot. Serve immediately.

Nutrition Info:

- Info Per Serving: Calories: 176.21; Fat:7.80 g ;Saturated fat:4.53 g ;Sodium: 228.89 mg

Poultry

Balsamic Blueberry Chicken

Servings: 2
Cooking Time: 25 Min
Ingredients:
- Aluminum foil
- ½ cup fresh blueberries
- 2 tbsp. pine nuts
- ¼ cup cilantro, chopped
- 2 tbsp. balsamic vinegar
- ¼ tsp ground black pepper
- 2 (4 oz) chicken breasts, butterflied

Directions:
1. Heat the olive oil in a medium-sized frying pan over medium Heat the oven to 375°F gas mark 5. Line a baking sheet with aluminum foil.
2. In a medium-sized mixing bowl, add the blueberries, pine nuts, cilantro, balsamic vinegar, and pepper, mix until well combined.
3. Place the chicken breasts on the baking sheet and pour the blueberry mixture on top.
4. Bake for 20 to 25 minutes, until the juices are caramelized, and the inside of the chicken has cooked through. Serve warm.

Nutrition Info:
- Info Per Serving: Calories: 212 ; Fat: 7 g ;Saturated fat:1 g ;Sodium: 58 mg

Chicken Paillards With Mushrooms

Servings: 4
Cooking Time: X
Ingredients:
- 4 (3-ounce) chicken breasts
- 3 tablespoons flour
- 1/8 teaspoon salt
- 1/8 teaspoon cayenne pepper
- ½ teaspoon dried marjoram leaves
- 2 tablespoons olive oil
- 4 shallots, minced
- 1 cup sliced button mushrooms
- 1 cup sliced cremini mushrooms
- ½ cup Low-Sodium Chicken Broth
- ¼ cup dry white wine
- 1 teaspoon Worcestershire sauce
- 1 tablespoon cornstarch

Directions:
1. Place chicken breasts between two sheets of waxed paper and pound until ¼" thick. On shallow plate, combine flour, salt, pepper, and marjoram. Dredge chicken in flour mixture to coat.
2. In large skillet, heat olive oil over medium heat. Add chicken; sauté on first side for 3 minutes, then carefully turn and cook for 1 minute longer. Remove to platter and cover to keep warm.
3. Add shallots and mushrooms to skillet; cook and stir for 4–5 minutes until tender. Meanwhile, in small bowl combine broth, wine, Worcestershire sauce, and cornstarch, and mix well. Add to mushroom mixture and bring to a boil.
4. Return chicken to skillet; cook until chicken is hot and sauce bubbles and thickens. Serve immediately over brown rice, couscous, or pasta.

Nutrition Info:
- Info Per Serving: Calories:270.13; Fat:8.25g ;Saturated fat:1.71 g ;Sodium: 167.63 mg

Piña Colada Chicken

Servings: 2
Cooking Time: 20 Min
Ingredients:
- Aluminum foil
- 2 (4 oz) chicken breasts, pounded flat
- 2 tsp unsweetened coconut flakes
- 1 (20 oz) can crushed pineapple, drained
- 1 cup green bell peppers, diced
- ¼ cup soy sauce

Directions:
1. Heat the oven to 400°F gas mark 6. Line a baking sheet with aluminum foil.
2. Place the chicken breasts on the baking sheet and top with coconut flakes.
3. Place the pineapple and green bell peppers around the chicken breasts.
4. Drizzle the chicken breasts with soy sauce and cook for 10 to 15 minutes, until the pineapple is caramelised, and the chicken is cooked through. Serve warm.

Nutrition Info:
- Info Per Serving: Calories: 327 ; Fat: 6 g ;Saturated fat: 1 g ;Sodium: 206 mg

Chicken Stir-fry With Napa Cabbage

Servings: 4
Cooking Time: X
Ingredients:
- 2 (5-ounce) boneless, skinless chicken breasts
- 2 tablespoons cornstarch
- 2 tablespoons lemon juice
- 1 tablespoon low-sodium soy sauce
- 1 cup Low-Sodium Chicken Broth
- 2 tablespoons peanut oil
- 4 cups shredded Napa cabbage
- 4 green onions, sliced
- 1 green bell pepper, sliced
- 1½ cups frozen edamame, thawed

Directions:
1. Cut chicken into 1″ pieces. In small bowl, combine cornstarch, lemon juice, soy sauce, and chicken broth. Add chicken and let stand for 15 minutes.
2. Heat oil in large skillet or wok. Drain chicken, reserving marinade. Add chicken to skillet; stir-fry until almost cooked, about 4 minutes. Remove chicken to a plate.
3. Add cabbage and green onions to skillet; stir fry until cabbage wilts, about 4 minutes. Add bell pepper and edamame; stir-fry for 3–5 minutes longer until hot.
4. Stir marinade and add to skillet along with chicken. Stir-fry until sauce bubbles and thickens and chicken is thoroughly cooked. Serve over hot cooked brown rice.

Nutrition Info:
- Info Per Serving: Calories:307.21; Fat: 14.90 g ;Saturated fat: 2.47 g ;Sodium:214.61 mg

Lime Chicken Wraps

Servings: 2
Cooking Time: X
Ingredients:
- 1 cup chicken breasts, cooked and chopped
- 1 cup low-sodium canned kidney beans, rinsed and drained
- ½ ripe avocado, diced
- 1 spring onion, finely chopped
- ½ lime, juiced and zested
- 1 tsp parsley, finely chopped
- ¼ tsp ground cumin
- 4 large iceberg lettuce leaves

Directions:
1. In a medium-sized mixing bowl, add the chicken breasts, kidney beans, avocado, spring onion, lime juice and zest, parsley, and d cumin, mix until well combined.
2. Divide the chicken filling evenly between the lettuce leaves and roll closed.
3. Serve cold.

Nutrition Info:
- Info Per Serving: Calories: 368 ; Fat: 11 g ;Saturated fat: 2 g ;Sodium: 58 mg

Nutty Coconut Chicken With Fruit Sauce

Servings: 4
Cooking Time: 15 Minutes
Ingredients:
- ¼ cup ground almonds
- ⅓ cup unsweetened flaked coconut
- ¼ cup coconut flour
- Pinch salt
- ⅛ teaspoon white pepper
- 1 egg white
- 1 (16-ounce) package chicken tenders
- 1 cup sliced strawberries
- 1 cup raspberries
- ⅓ cup unsweetened white grape juice
- 1 tablespoon lemon juice
- ½ teaspoon dried thyme leaves
- ⅓ cup dried cherries

Directions:
1. Preheat the oven to 400°F. Place a wire rack on a baking sheet.
2. In a shallow plate, combine the ground almonds, flaked coconut, coconut flour, salt, and white pepper, and mix well.
3. In a shallow bowl, beat the egg white just until foamy.
4. Dip the chicken tenders into the egg white, then into the almond mixture to coat. Place on the wire rack as you work.
5. Bake the chicken tenders for 14 to 16 minutes or until the chicken is cooked to 165°F when tested with a meat thermometer.
6. While the chicken is baking, in a food processor or blender, combine the strawberries, raspberries, grape juice, lemon juice, and thyme leaves and process or blend until smooth.
7. Pour the mixture into a small saucepan, and add the dried cherries. Bring to a simmer over medium heat. Simmer for 3 minutes, then remove the pan from the heat and set aside.
8. Serve the chicken with the warm fruit sauce.

Nutrition Info:
- Info Per Serving: Calories: 281 ; Fat : 8 g ;Saturated fat: 3 g ;Sodium: 124 mg

Crunchy Chicken Coleslaw Salad

Servings: 4
Cooking Time: 7 Minutes
Ingredients:
- 3 (6-ounce) boneless, skinless chicken breasts, cubed
- Pinch salt
- ⅛ teaspoon white pepper
- 1 teaspoon toasted sesame oil
- ¼ cup low-fat mayonnaise
- ¼ cup low-sodium chicken broth
- 2 tablespoons fresh lemon juice
- 1 tablespoon low-sodium yellow mustard
- 2 tablespoons chopped fresh dill
- 4 cups shredded red cabbage
- 1 small yellow summer squash, sliced
- 1 small carrot, shredded
- 2 tablespoons sunflower seeds

Directions:
1. Sprinkle the chicken with the salt and pepper.
2. Heat the sesame oil in a large nonstick skillet. Add the chicken and cook, stirring frequently, until lightly browned and cooked to 165°F when tested with a meat thermometer, about 5 to 7 minutes. Remove from the skillet and set aside.
3. In a large bowl, combine the mayonnaise, chicken broth, lemon juice, mustard, and dill and mix well.
4. Add the cabbage, squash, and carrot to the dressing in the bowl and toss.
5. Add the chicken to the salad and toss.
6. Sprinkle with the sunflower seeds and serve.

Nutrition Info:
- Info Per Serving: Calories: 256; Fat : 9 g ;Saturated fat: 2 g ;Sodium: 169 mg

Tandoori Turkey Pizzas

Servings: 4
Cooking Time: 18 Minutes
Ingredients:
- 4 (6½-inch) whole-wheat pita breads
- 1 teaspoon olive oil
- 1 onion, chopped
- 4 cloves garlic, minced
- ½ pound ground turkey
- 1 (8-ounce) can no-salt-added tomato sauce
- 2 teaspoons curry powder
- ½ teaspoon smoked paprika
- ¼ teaspoon ground cumin
- ⅛ teaspoon cayenne pepper
- ¼ cup crumbled feta cheese
- 3 tablespoons low-fat plain Greek yogurt

Directions:
1. Preheat the oven to 425°F. Place the pita breads on a baking sheet lined with aluminum foil and set aside.
2. In a large skillet, heat the olive oil over medium heat. Add the onion and garlic and cook, stirring frequently, for 2 minutes.
3. Add the ground turkey and sauté, breaking up the meat. Cook for 5 minutes or until the turkey is no longer pink.
4. Add the tomato sauce, curry powder, paprika, cumin, and cayenne pepper to the sauce and bring to a simmer. Simmer over low heat for 1 minute.
5. Top the pita "pizzas" evenly with the turkey mixture. Sprinkle each with the feta cheese.
6. Bake for 10 to 12 minutes or until the pizzas are hot. Drizzle each pizza with the yogurt and serve immediately.

Nutrition Info:
- Info Per Serving: Calories: 308 ; Fat : 6 g ;Saturated fat: 2 g ;Sodium: 779 mg

Chicken Rice

Servings: 2
Cooking Time: 25 Min
Ingredients:
- 1 cup brown basmati rice, cooked
- 1 cup chicken breast, cooked and chopped
- 1 cup spinach, cooked and shredded
- ½ cup low-sodium canned garbanzo beans, drained and rinsed
- 4 tbsp. lemon and herb vinaigrette, divided
- 1 large carrot, peeled and grated
- 1 large red bell pepper, diced
- 1 large green bell pepper, diced
- 1 cup frozen peas, cooked
- ½ cup frozen corn, cooked
- ¼ cup pine nuts, toasted for garnish

Directions:
1. In a medium-sized mixing bowl, add the basmati rice, chicken breasts, spinach, garbanzo beans and 2 tbsp. of the lemon and herb vinaigrette, mix to combine.
2. Divide the rice mixture between two large bowls and arrange the carrot, red bell pepper, green bell pepper, peas, and corn in the bowls and drizzle with the remaining lemon and herb vinaigrette.
3. Top with pine nuts and serve.

Nutrition Info:
- Info Per Serving: Calories: 503 ; Fat: 21 g ;Saturated fat:3 g ;Sodium: 187 mg

Turkey Oat Patties

Servings: 6
Cooking Time: 30 Min
Ingredients:
- Aluminum foil
- 1 lb. lean ground turkey
- ½ cup rolled oats
- ¼ cup sun-dried tomatoes julienne cut, drained
- ¼ cup brown onion, finely chopped
- ¼ cup parsley, finely chopped
- 1 tbsp. garlic, crushed
- 6 whole-wheat hamburger buns
- 1 ripe avocado, peeled, pitted, and mashed
- 6 iceberg lettuce leaves
- 6 Roma tomato slices
- Hamburger dill pickle chips

Directions:
1. Preheat the oven to broil. Line a baking sheet with aluminum foil.
2. In a large-sized mixing bowl, add the turkey, oats, sun-dried tomatoes, onion, parsley, and garlic, mix to combine. Shape into 6 patties.
3. Place the turkey patties on the baking sheet, and broil for 3 to 4 minutes on each side, until fully cooked and the juices run clear.
4. Meanwhile, prepare a self-serving platter with the buns, mashed avocado, lettuce leaves, tomato slices, and the dill pickle chips. Assemble the way you like.

Nutrition Info:
- Info Per Serving: Calories: 366 ; Fat: 15g;Saturated fat: 3 g ;Sodium: 52 mg

Lemon Tarragon Turkey Medallions

Servings: 4
Cooking Time: 10 Minutes
Ingredients:
- 1 pound turkey tenderloin
- Pinch salt
- ⅛ teaspoon lemon pepper
- 2 tablespoons cornstarch
- 1 teaspoon dried tarragon leaves
- ¼ cup fresh lemon juice
- ½ cup low-sodium chicken stock
- 1 teaspoon grated fresh lemon zest
- 2 teaspoons olive oil

Directions:
1. Cut the turkey tenderloin crosswise into ½-inch slices. Sprinkle with the salt and lemon pepper.
2. In a small bowl, combine the cornstarch, tarragon, lemon juice, chicken stock, and lemon zest, and mix well.
3. Heat the olive oil in a large nonstick skillet over medium heat.
4. Add the turkey tenderloins. Cook for 2 minutes, and then turn and cook for another 2 minutes.
5. Add the lemon juice mixture to the skillet. Cook, stirring frequently, until the sauce boils and thickens and the turkey is cooked to 165°F on a meat thermometer. Serve immediately.

Nutrition Info:
- Info Per Serving: Calories: 169 ; Fat :3 g ;Saturated fat: 1 g ;Sodium: 77 mg

Turkey Curry With Fruit

Servings: 6
Cooking Time: X
Ingredients:
- 6 (4-ounce) turkey cutlets
- 1 tablespoon flour
- 1 tablespoon plus
- 1 teaspoon curry powder, divided
- 1 tablespoon olive oil
- 2 pears, chopped
- 1 apple, chopped ½ cup raisins
- 1 tablespoon sugar
- 1/8 teaspoon salt
- 1/3 cup apricot jam

Directions:
1. Preheat oven to 350ºF. Spray a cookie sheet with sides with nonstick cooking spray. Arrange cutlets on prepared cookie sheet. In small bowl, combine flour, 1 tablespoon curry powder, and olive oil and mix well. Spread evenly over cutlets.
2. In medium bowl, combine pears, apple, raisins, sugar, salt, 1 teaspoon curry powder, and apricot jam, and mix well. Divide this mixture over the turkey cutlets.
3. Bake for 35–45 minutes or until turkey is thoroughly cooked and fruit is hot and caramelized. Serve immediately.

Nutrition Info:
- Info Per Serving: Calories: 371.52; Fat: 11.15 g ;Saturated fat: 2.80 g ;Sodium: 121.35 mg

Grilled Turkey And Veggie Kabobs

Servings: 4
Cooking Time: 10 Minutes
Ingredients:
- 1 pound turkey tenderloin
- Pinch salt
- ⅛ teaspoon cayenne pepper
- 1 yellow summer squash, cut into ½-inch slices
- 1 orange bell pepper, seeded and cut into 1-inch cubes
- 1 red bell pepper, seeded and cut into 1-inch cubes
- 3 scallions, cut into 2-inch pieces
- ¼ cup apple jelly
- 2 tablespoons fresh lemon juice
- 1 tablespoon butter
- 1 tablespoon low-sodium mustard
- 1 teaspoon dried oregano leaves

Directions:
1. Prepare and preheat the grill to medium heat.
2. Cut the turkey into 1-inch cubes, put on a plate, and sprinkle with the salt and cayenne pepper.
3. Thread the turkey cubes, alternating with the squash, orange bell pepper, red bell pepper, and scallion, onto kabob skewers.
4. In a small saucepan, combine the apple jelly, lemon juice, and butter. Heat over low heat until the apple jelly melts and the mixture is smooth, about 2 minutes. Stir in the mustard and oregano.
5. Place the kabobs on the hot grill and brush with some of the apple jelly mixture. Cover and grill for 4 minutes.
6. Uncover, turn the kabobs, and brush with more of the apple jelly mixture. Cover and grill for 3 minutes.
7. Uncover the grill and turn the kabobs, brushing with the remaining apple jelly mixture, and cook until the turkey registers 165°F on a meat thermometer, 2 to 3 minutes longer. Use all of the apple jelly mixture; if any is left, discard it.

Nutrition Info:
- Info Per Serving: Calories: 232 ; Fat : 5 g ;Saturated fat: 2 g ;Sodium: 194 mg

Sautéed Chicken With Roasted Garlic Sauce

Servings: 4
Cooking Time: X
Ingredients:
- 1 head Roasted Garlic
- 1/3 cup Low-Sodium Chicken Broth
- ½ teaspoon dried oregano leaves
- 4 (4-ounce) boneless, skinless chicken breasts
- ¼ cup flour
- 1/8 teaspoon salt
- 1/8 teaspoon pepper
- ¼ teaspoon paprika
- 2 tablespoons olive oil

Directions:
1. Squeeze garlic cloves from the skins and combine in small saucepan with chicken broth and oregano leaves.
2. On shallow plate, combine flour, salt, pepper, and paprika. Dip chicken into this mixture to coat.
3. In large skillet, heat 2 tablespoons olive oil. At the same time, place the saucepan with the garlic mixture over medium heat. Add the chicken to the hot olive oil; cook for 5 minutes without moving. Then carefully turn chicken and cook for 4–7 minutes longer until chicken is thoroughly cooked.
4. Stir garlic sauce with wire whisk until blended. Serve with the chicken.

Nutrition Info:
- Info Per Serving: Calories: 267.01; Fat: 7.78g ;Saturated fat:1.65 g ;Sodium: 158.61 mg

"butter" Chicken

Servings: 4
Cooking Time: 12 Minutes
Ingredients:
- 4 (6-ounce) boneless, skinless chicken breasts, cubed
- 2 tablespoons fresh lemon juice
- 2 teaspoons curry powder
- 1 teaspoon chili powder
- ⅛ teaspoon black pepper
- 2 teaspoons olive oil
- 1 onion, chopped
- 4 cloves garlic, minced
- ½ cup low-fat coconut milk
- ½ cup low-fat plain Greek yogurt
- 2 tablespoons no-salt-added tomato paste
- 1 tablespoon cornstarch

Directions:
1. In a large bowl, combine the chicken with the lemon juice, curry powder, chili powder, and black pepper, and mix with your hands, rubbing the spices into the chicken. Set aside.
2. In a large nonstick skillet, heat the olive oil over medium heat.
3. Add the onion and garlic, and sauté for 4 to 5 minutes, until tender.
4. Add the chicken and sauté, stirring frequently, until the chicken starts to brown, about 4 minutes.
5. Meanwhile, in a small bowl, combine the coconut milk, yogurt, tomato paste, and cornstarch, and mix well with a whisk.
6. Add the coconut milk mixture to the skillet. Simmer 4 to 5 minutes or until the sauce is thickened and the chicken registers 165°F on a meat thermometer. Serve hot.

Nutrition Info:
- Info Per Serving: Calories: 308 ; Fat : 8 g ;Saturated fat: 3 g ;Sodium: 144 mg

Moroccan Chicken

Servings: 4
Cooking Time: 15 Minutes
Ingredients:
- 3 (4-ounce) boneless, skinless chicken thighs, cubed
- 1 teaspoon smoked paprika
- ½ teaspoon ground cinnamon
- ½ teaspoon ground cumin
- ⅛ teaspoon ground ginger
- 1 cup low-sodium chicken broth
- 2 tablespoons fresh lemon juice
- 1 tablespoon cornstarch
- 1 teaspoon olive oil
- 1 onion, chopped
- 3 cloves garlic, minced
- 2 cups sugar snap peas
- 1 cup shredded carrots

Directions:
1. Put the cubed chicken in a medium bowl. Sprinkle with the paprika, cinnamon, cumin, and ginger, and work the spices into the meat. Set aside.
2. In a small bowl, combine the chicken broth, lemon juice, and cornstarch and mix well. Set aside.
3. Heat the olive oil in a large nonstick skillet over medium-high heat. Add the chicken thighs, and sauté for 5 minutes or until the chicken starts to brown. Remove the chicken from the pan and set aside.
4. Add the onion and garlic to the skillet, and sauté for 3 minutes.
5. Add the sugar snap peas and carrots to the skillet and sauté for 2 minutes.
6. Return the chicken to the skillet and stir. Add the chicken broth mixture, bring to a simmer, and turn down the heat to low. Simmer 3 to 4 minutes or until the sauce thickens, the vegetables are tender, and the chicken is cooked to 165°F on a meat thermometer. Serve hot.

Nutrition Info:
- Info Per Serving: Calories: 165 ; Fat : 5 g ;Saturated fat: 1 g ;Sodium: 112 mg

Chicken Pesto

Servings: 6
Cooking Time: X
Ingredients:

- 1 cup packed fresh basil leaves
- ¼ cup toasted chopped hazelnuts
- 2 cloves garlic, chopped
- 2 tablespoons olive oil
- 1 tablespoons water
- ¼ cup grated Parmesan cheese
- ½ cup Low-Sodium Chicken Broth
- 12 ounces boneless, skinless chicken breasts
- 1 (12-ounce) package angel hair pasta

Directions:

1. Bring a large pot of salted water to a boil. In blender or food processor, combine basil, hazelnuts, and garlic. Blend or process until very finely chopped. Add olive oil and water; blend until a paste forms. Then blend in Parmesan cheese; set aside.
2. In large skillet, bring chicken broth to a simmer over medium heat. Cut chicken into strips and add to broth. Cook for 4 minutes, then add the pasta to the boiling water.
3. Cook pasta for 3–4 minutes according to package directions, until al dente. Drain and add to chicken mixture; cook and stir for 1 minute until chicken is thoroughly cooked. Add basil mixture, remove from heat, and stir until a sauce forms. Serve immediately.

Nutrition Info:

- Info Per Serving: Calories: 373.68; Fat: 11.06 g ;Saturated fat: 2.01 g ;Sodium: 108.92 mg

Turkey Cutlets Parmesan

Servings: 6
Cooking Time: X
Ingredients:

- 1 egg white
- ¼ cup dry breadcrumbs
- 1/8 teaspoon pepper
- 4 tablespoons grated Parmesan cheese, divided
- 6 (4-ounce) turkey cutlets
- 2 tablespoons olive oil
- 1 (15-ounce) can no-salt tomato sauce
- 1 teaspoon dried Italian seasoning
- ½ cup finely shredded part-skim mozzarella cheese

Directions:

1. Preheat oven to 350ºF. Spray a 2-quart baking dish with nonstick cooking spray and set aside.
2. In shallow bowl, beat egg white until foamy. On plate, combine breadcrumbs, pepper, and 2 tablespoons Parmesan. Dip the turkey cutlets into the egg white, then into the breadcrumb mixture, turning to coat.
3. In large saucepan, heat olive oil over medium heat. Add turkey cutlets; brown on both sides, about 2–3 minutes per side. Place in prepared baking dish. Add tomato sauce and Italian seasoning to saucepan; bring to a boil.
4. Pour sauce over cutlets in baking pan and top with mozzarella cheese and remaining 2 tablespoons Parmesan. Bake for 25–35 minutes or until sauce bubbles and cheese melts and begins to brown. Serve with pasta, if desired.

Nutrition Info:

- Info Per Serving: Calories: 275.49; Fat: 10.98 g ;Saturated fat:3.43 g ;Sodium: 229.86 mg

Italian Chicken Bake

Servings: 4
Cooking Time: 25 Min
Ingredients:
- 1 lb. chicken breasts, halved lengthwise into 4 pieces
- ½ tsp garlic powder
- ½ tsp fine sea salt
- ¼ tsp ground black pepper
- ¼ tsp Italian seasoning
- ½ cup basil, finely chopped
- 4 part-skim mozzarella cheese slices
- 2 large Roma tomatoes, finely chopped

Directions:
1. Heat the oven to 400°F gas mark 6.
2. Season the cut chicken breasts with garlic powder, salt, pepper and Italian seasoning.
3. Place the seasoned chicken breasts on a baking sheet. Bake for 18 to 22 minutes, or until the chicken breasts are cooked through. Remove from the oven and set it to broil on high.
4. Evenly place the basil, 1 mozzarella slice and tomatoes on each chicken breast.
5. Return the baking sheet to the oven and broil for 2 to 3 minutes, until the cheese has melted and browned.
6. Remove from the oven and serve hot.

Nutrition Info:
- Info Per Serving: Calories: 239 ; Fat: 9 g ;Saturated fat: 4 g ;Sodium: 524 mg

Basil Chicken Meatballs

Servings: 20
Cooking Time: 10 Minutes
Ingredients:
- 1 egg white
- ⅓ cup gluten-free (or whole-wheat) bread crumbs
- ½ cup low-sodium chicken broth, divided
- 1 tablespoon fresh lemon juice
- 1 tablespoon freeze-dried chopped chives
- 3 tablespoons minced fresh basil leaves
- ⅛ teaspoon garlic powder
- Pinch salt
- Pinch black pepper
- ¾ pound ground white chicken breast meat

Directions:
1. In a medium bowl, combine the egg white, bread crumbs, 2 tablespoons of the chicken broth, lemon juice, chives, basil, garlic powder, salt, and pepper, and mix well.
2. Add the ground chicken and mix gently but thoroughly until combined.
3. Form into 20 meatballs, about 1 inch in diameter.
4. Heat the remaining 6 tablespoons of the chicken broth in a large nonstick skillet over medium-high heat.
5. Gently add the chicken meatballs in a single layer. Let cook for 5 minutes, then carefully turn and cook another 3 minutes.
6. Lower the heat as the broth reduces, and continue cooking the meatballs, gently shaking the pan occasionally, until the broth has mostly evaporated and the meatballs are browned and cooked to 165°F as tested with a meat thermometer, another 2 to 3 minutes.

Nutrition Info:
- Info Per Serving: Calories: 130 ; Fat : 3 g ;Saturated fat: 1 g ;Sodium: 162 mg

Lime Turkey Skewers

Servings: 4
Cooking Time: 15 Min

Ingredients:

- 1 lb. boneless, skinless turkey breasts, cut into chunks
- 1 lime, juiced
- 2 tbsp. avocado oil, plus 1 tbsp.
- 2 tbsp. garlic, minced
- 1 tsp dried thyme
- 1 tsp dried dill
- ½ tsp fine sea salt
- ¼ tsp ground black pepper

Directions:

1. In a medium-sized mixing bowl, add the turkey breasts, lime juice, avocado oil, garlic, thyme, dill, salt and pepper, mix to combine. Rest for 30 minutes in the fridge.
2. Thread the marinated turkey chunks onto 8 skewers.
3. Heat 1 tbsp. of avocado oil in a heavy-bottom pan over medium-high heat.
4. Place the skewers gently in the pan and fry for 5 to 7 minutes, flip, and cook for 5 to 8 minutes, or until the turkey is cooked through and no longer pink inside. Remove from the heat and serve.

Nutrition Info:

- Info Per Serving: Calories: 205 ; Fat: 10 g ;Saturated fat: 2 g ;Sodium: 343 mg

Cashew Chicken

Servings: 2
Cooking Time: 5 Min

Ingredients:

- 2 tsp olive oil
- 2 tsp garlic, minced, divided
- ½ cup red onion, chopped
- 8 oz ground chicken
- 1 tsp ginger, grated
- 3 tbsp. unsalted cashew butter
- 4 tbsp. water
- 6 large green leaf lettuce leaves
- ½ cup unsalted cashew nuts, roughly chopped

Directions:

1. Heat the olive oil in a medium-sized frying pan over medium heat. Add the 1 tsp garlic and onion, cook for 1 to 2 minutes, until translucent.
2. Add the chicken and separate using a fork. Continue mixing for 5 minutes until lightly golden and cooked through.
3. In a small-sized mixing bowl, add the ginger, remaining 1 tsp garlic, cashew butter, and water, mix to combine.
4. Add the cashew mixture to the ground chicken. Cook for 1 minute until all flavors have combined.
5. Divide the cashew chicken mixture into the lettuce cups and serve topped with the cashew nuts.

Nutrition Info:

- Info Per Serving: Calories: 414 ; Fat: 21 g ;Saturated fat: 4 g ;Sodium: 211 mg

Pork And Beef Mains

Sirloin Steak With Root Vegetables

Servings: X
Cooking Time: 40 Minutes
Ingredients:
- 1 (10-ounce) sirloin steak, fat trimmed
- Sea salt
- Freshly ground black pepper
- 2 carrots, cut into 1-inch chunks
- 2 parsnip, cut into 1-inch chunks
- 1 small celeriac, peeled and cut into 1-inch chunks
- 1 small sweet potato, peeled and cut into 1-inch chunks
- 6 beets, peeled and halved
- 1 tablespoon olive oil, plus extra for drizzling

Directions:
1. Preheat the oven to 400°F.
2. Line a sheet pan with foil and set aside.
3. Season the steak with salt and pepper and set aside.
4. Spread the veggies on the sheet pan, leaving room for the steak. Season them lightly with salt and pepper and drizzle with 1 tablespoon olive oil.
5. Roast the veggies until they are lightly caramelized and tender, about 30 minutes.
6. Remove the sheet pan from the oven and add the steak.
7. Increase the oven temperature to broil.
8. Place the sheet pan into the oven and broil until the steak is browned, 4 to 5 minutes per side for medium-rare, or until it reaches your desired doneness.
9. Serve.

Nutrition Info:
- Info Per Serving: Calories: 565 ; Fat: 26 g ;Saturated fat: 8 g ;Sodium: 274 mg

Pork Quesadillas

Servings: 6
Cooking Time: X
Ingredients:
- 1/3 cup low-fat sour cream
- 1 cup shredded part-skim mozzarella cheese
- 1 cup chopped Mustard Pork Tenderloin (below)
- 1 avocado, chopped
- 1 jalapeño pepper, minced
- 10 (6-inch) corn tortillas
- 2 tablespoons olive oil

Directions:
1. In medium bowl, combine sour cream, cheese, pork tenderloin, avocado, and jalapeño pepper and mix gently.
2. Divide mixture among half the tortillas, placing the remaining half of tortillas on top to make sandwiches. Heat griddle and brush with olive oil. Place quesadillas on the griddle; cover and grill for 2–3 minutes on each side until tortillas are crisp and cheese is melted. Cut into quarters and serve.

Nutrition Info:
- Info Per Serving: Calories: 315.36 ; Fat:16.67 g ;Saturated fat:5.55 g ;Sodium:161.17 mg

Pork Scallops With Spinach

Servings: 6
Cooking Time: X
Ingredients:
- 3 tablespoons flour
- 1/8 teaspoon salt
- 1/8 teaspoon pepper
- 6 (3-ounce) pork scallops
- 2 tablespoons olive oil
- 1 onion, chopped
- 1 (10-ounce) package frozen chopped spinach, thawed
- 1 tablespoon flour
- ½ teaspoon celery seed
- 1/3 cup nonfat light cream
- 1/3 cup part-skim ricotta cheese
- ½ cup dried breadcrumbs, divided
- 2 tablespoons grated Romano cheese

Directions:
1. Preheat oven to 350ºF. On plate, combine 3 tablespoons flour, salt, and pepper and mix well. Pound pork scallops, if necessary, to A1/8" thickness.
2. Heat olive oil in nonstick pan over medium-high heat. Dredge pork in flour mixture and sauté in pan, turning once, until just browned, about 1 minute per side. Remove to a baking dish.
3. Add onion to pan; cook and stir for 3 minutes. Drain spinach well and add to pan; cook and stir until liquid evaporates. Add flour and celery seed; cook and stir for 1 minute.
4. Stir in light cream; cook and stir until thickened, about 3 minutes. Remove from heat and add ricotta cheese and half of the breadcrumbs.
5. Divide spinach mixture on top of pork in baking dish. Top with remaining breadcrumbs and Romano. Bake for 10–15 minutes or until pork is tender and thoroughly cooked. Serve immediately.

Nutrition Info:
- Info Per Serving: Calories: 298.66; Fat: 12.60 g ;Saturated fat:4.08 g ;Sodium: 303.25 mg

Cowboy Steak With Chimichurri Sauce

Servings: 4–6
Cooking Time: X
Ingredients:
- 1 cup chopped parsley
- ¼ cup minced fresh oregano leaves
- ¼ cup extra-virgin olive oil
- 2 tablespoons lemon juice
- 3 tablespoons sherry vinegar
- 6 cloves garlic, minced
- 1/8 teaspoon salt
- ¼ teaspoon pepper
- 1 pound flank steak
- 2 tablespoons red wine
- 2 tablespoons olive oil

Directions:
1. In blender or food processor, combine parsley, oregano, olive oil, lemon juice, sherry vinegar, garlic, salt, and pepper; blend or process until smooth. Pour into small bowl, cover, and refrigerate until ready to use.
2. Pierce flank steak all over with a fork. Place in large heavy-duty zip-close freezer bag and add red wine and olive oil. Seal bag and squish to mix. Place in pan and refrigerate for 8–12 hours.
3. When ready to eat, prepare and preheat grill. Grill steak for 6–10 minutes, turning once, until desired doneness. Remove from grill and let stand, covered, for 10 minutes. Slice thinly against the grain and serve with the Chimichurri Sauce.

Nutrition Info:
- Info Per Serving: Calories:244.50; Fat:18.59 g ;Saturated fat: 5.20 g ;Sodium: 117.31 mg

Meatball Pizza

Servings: 6
Cooking Time: X
Ingredients:

- 1 Whole-Grain Pizza Crust , prebaked
- 1 tablespoon olive oil
- 1 onion, chopped
- 1 green bell pepper, chopped
- ½ cup shredded carrots
- 1 (6-ounce) can no-salt tomato paste
- 2 tablespoons mustard
- ¼ cup water
- 12 plain Sirloin Meatballs , baked
- 1 cup shredded extra-sharp Cheddar cheese
- ½ cup shredded part-skim mozzarella cheese

Directions:

1. Preheat oven to 400ºF. In medium saucepan, heat olive oil over medium heat. Add onion, bell pepper, and carrots; cook and stir until crisp-tender, about 5 minutes. Add tomato paste, mustard, and water and bring to a simmer. Simmer, stirring frequently, for 5 minutes.
2. Spread the sauce over the pizza crust. Cut the meatballs in half and arrange on the pizza. Sprinkle with Cheddar and mozzarella cheeses.
3. Bake for 20–30 minutes or until crust is golden brown, pizza is hot, and cheese is melted and bubbling. Let stand for 5 minutes, then serve.

Nutrition Info:

- Info Per Serving: Calories:437.80; Fat: 15.85 g ;Saturated fat: 6.29g ;Sodium: 432.76 mg

Pork Bahmi Goreng

Servings: X
Cooking Time: 30 Minutes
Ingredients:

- 2 teaspoons olive oil
- 1 (8-ounce) pork tenderloin, cut into ½-inch cubes
- 2 leeks, white and green parts, finely sliced
- ½ sweet onion, thinly sliced
- ½ small head of cabbage, finely shredded
- 1 tablespoon low-sodium tamari sauce
- 2 teaspoons sambal oelek or your favorite chili sauce
- Juice of ½ lime
- 1 teaspoon minced garlic
- 1 teaspoon peeled, grated ginger
- ¼ teaspoon ground cumin
- 4 ounces dry rice noodles

Directions:

1. In a large skillet, warm the oil over medium-high heat.
2. Add the pork and sauté until it is cooked through, 8 to 10 minutes. Remove the pork with a slotted spoon and set aside.
3. Add the leeks and onions to the skillet and sauté until softened, about 5 minutes.
4. Stir in the cabbage and sauté until tender, 8 to 10 minutes.
5. Add the pork back to the skillet and stir in the tamari, sambal oelek, lime juice, garlic, ginger, and cumin. Sauté for 5 minutes, then remove from the heat and set aside while you prepare the noodles.
6. Cook the rice noodles according to package directions. Drain and add to the skillet.
7. Toss to warm and combine all of the ingredients, and serve.

Nutrition Info:

- Info Per Serving: Calories: 481 ; Fat: 8 g ;Saturated fat: 2 g ;Sodium: 482 mg

Pork Goulash

Servings: 4
Cooking Time: 15 Minutes
Ingredients:
- ½ pound lean ground pork
- 2 onions, chopped
- 8 ounces sliced button mushrooms
- 4 cloves garlic, minced
- 3 stalks celery, sliced
- ½ cup grated carrot
- 2 teaspoons smoked paprika
- Pinch salt
- ⅛ teaspoon white pepper
- 1 (14-ounce) can no-salt-added diced tomatoes
- 1 (8-ounce) can no-salt-added tomato sauce
- 2 tablespoons tomato paste
- ½ cup water
- 1 cup whole-wheat orzo

Directions:
1. In a large skillet over medium-high, sauté the pork, onions, mushrooms, garlic, celery, and carrot for 4 minutes, stirring to break up the pork, until the meat is almost cooked through.
2. Add the paprika, salt, white pepper, tomatoes, tomato sauce, tomato paste, and water, and bring to a simmer. Simmer for 1 minute.
3. Add the orzo to the skillet and stir, making sure that the pasta is covered by liquid. Simmer for 10 to 12 minutes or until the pasta is cooked al dente. Serve immediately.

Nutrition Info:
- Info Per Serving: Calories:299 ; Fat:7 g ;Saturated fat: 2 g ;Sodium: 128 mg

Sirloin Meatballs In Sauce

Servings: 6
Cooking Time: X
Ingredients:
- 1 tablespoon olive oil
- 3 cloves garlic, minced
- ½ cup minced onion
- 2 egg whites
- ½ cup dry breadcrumbs
- ¼ cup grated Parmesan cheese
- ½ teaspoon crushed fennel seeds
- ½ teaspoon dried oregano leaves
- 2 teaspoons Worcestershire sauce
- 1/8 teaspoon pepper
- 1/8 teaspoon crushed red pepper flakes
- 1 pound 95% lean ground sirloin
- 1 recipe Spaghetti Sauce

Directions:
1. In small saucepan, heat olive oil over medium heat. Add garlic and onion; cook and stir until tender, about 5 minutes. Remove from heat and place in large mixing bowl.
2. Add egg whites, breadcrumbs, Parmesan, fennel, oregano, Worcestershire sauce, pepper, and pepper flakes and mix well. Add sirloin; mix gently but thoroughly until combined. Form into 12 meatballs.
3. In large nonstick saucepan, place Spaghetti Sauce and bring to a simmer. Carefully add meatballs to sauce. Return to a simmer, partially cover, and simmer for 15–25 minutes or until meatballs are thoroughly cooked.

Nutrition Info:
- Info Per Serving: Calories: 367.93; Fat: 13.56 g ;Saturated fat: 3.91 g;Sodium: 305.47 mg

Whole-wheat Spaghetti And Meatballs

Servings: 6–8
Cooking Time: X
Ingredients:

- 1 recipe Sirloin Meatballs in Sauce
- 1 (8-ounce) can no-salt tomato sauce
- ½ cup grated carrots
- 1 (16-ounce) package whole-wheat spaghetti
- ½ cup grated Parmesan cheese, divided

Directions:

1. Bring a large pot of water to a boil. Prepare the Sirloin Meatballs in Sauce, adding tomato sauce and grated carrots to the sauce. Simmer until meatballs are cooked.
2. Cook spaghetti in water according to package directions or until almost al dente. Drain spaghetti, reserving ¼ cup cooking water. Add spaghetti to meatballs in sauce along with ¼ cup of the cheese. Simmer, stirring gently, for 5–6 minutes or until pasta is al dente, adding reserved cooking water if necessary for desired sauce consistency. Sprinkle with the remaining ¼ cup Parmesan cheese and serve immediately.

Nutrition Info:

- Info Per Serving: Calories: 386.78; Fat:12.34 g ;Saturated fat: 4.08 g ;Sodium: 444.23 mg

Thin Pork Chops With Mushrooms And Herbs

Servings: 4
Cooking Time: X
Ingredients:

- 3 tablespoons flour
- ¼ teaspoon salt
- 1/8 teaspoon white pepper
- 1 teaspoon dried thyme leaves
- 4 (3-ounce) boneless pork chops
- 2 tablespoons olive oil
- 2 shallots, minced
- 1 cup sliced cremini mushrooms
- 1 tablespoon fresh rosemary leaves, minced
- ¼ cup dry sherry

Directions:

1. On shallow plate, combine flour, salt, pepper, and thyme leaves and mix well. Place pork between two sheets of waxed paper and pound until ½" thick. Dredge pork chops in mixture, shaking off excess.
2. Heat olive oil in large skillet over medium heat. Add pork chops; brown on first side without moving, about 4 minutes.
3. Turn pork and add shallots and mushrooms to the pan. Cook for 3 minutes, then remove pork from pan. Stir vegetables, scraping pan to remove drippings.
4. Add rosemary and sherry to pan and bring to a boil. Return pork to skillet, lower heat, and simmer pork for 2–4 minutes longer until pork is very light pink. Serve immediately.

Nutrition Info:

- Info Per Serving: Calories:238.91 ; Fat:14.92 g ;Saturated fat: 3.97 g ;Sodium:392.89 mg

Simple Pork Burgers

Servings: X
Cooking Time: 15 Minutes
Ingredients:

- ½ pound extra-lean ground pork
- 1 large egg white
- 1 scallion, white parts only, chopped
- ¼ cup ground almonds
- ¼ teaspoon minced garlic
- ⅛ teaspoon allspice
- Sea salt
- Freshly ground black pepper

Directions:

1. Preheat a grill to medium-high heat.
2. In a medium bowl, thoroughly mix together the pork, egg white, scallion, almonds, garlic, and allspice. Season the mixture with salt and pepper.
3. Form the mixture into 2 burgers.
4. Place the burgers on the grill and cook until they are just cooked through, 7 to 8 minutes per side, depending on the thickness of the patties.
5. Serve with your favorite toppings.

Nutrition Info:

- Info Per Serving: Calories: 243 ; Fat: 13 g ;Saturated fat: 3 g ;Sodium: 83 mg

Pork And Fennel Stir Fry

Servings: 4
Cooking Time: 10 Minutes
Ingredients:

- 1 fennel bulb
- 1½ cups low-sodium chicken broth
- 1 tablespoon rice wine vinegar
- 1 tablespoon honey
- 2 tablespoons cornstarch
- 1 teaspoon soy sauce
- 12 ounces boneless top loin pork chops
- Pinch salt
- ⅛ teaspoon white pepper
- 2 teaspoons olive oil
- 8 ounces cremini mushrooms, sliced
- 3 stalks celery, sliced
- 2 cloves garlic, minced

Directions:

1. To prepare the fennel, trim the root end and cut off the stalk. Cut the bulb in half and peel off the outer skin. Slice the fennel thinly crosswise, and set aside. Finely slice the stalks, if desired. Cut some of the fennel fronds into tiny pieces with kitchen scissors, and set aside.
2. In a small bowl, combine the chicken broth, rice wine vinegar, honey, cornstarch, and soy sauce, and whisk to combine. Set aside.
3. Trim excess fat from the pork chops, and cut into 1-inch pieces. Sprinkle with the salt and white pepper.
4. Heat the olive oil in a large nonstick skillet or wok over medium-high heat. Add the pork and stir-fry until lightly browned, about 3 minutes. Remove the pork to a clean plate.
5. Add the fennel, fennel stalks if using, mushrooms, celery, and garlic to the skillet, and stir-fry for 3 to 4 minutes or until crisp-tender.
6. Stir the broth mixture, add it to the skillet, and bring to a simmer.
7. Add the pork and stir-fry 2 to 3 minutes or until the pork is cooked to at least 150°F on a meat thermometer and the sauce is thickened. Sprinkle with the reserved fennel fronds and serve immediately.

Nutrition Info:

- Info Per Serving: Calories: 204 ; Fat: 7 g ;Saturated fat: 2 g ;Sodium: 324 mg

Steak-and-pepper Kabobs

Servings: 4
Cooking Time: X
Ingredients:

- 2 tablespoons brown sugar
- ½ teaspoon garlic powder
- 1/8 teaspoon cayenne pepper
- ¼ teaspoon onion salt
- ½ teaspoon chili powder
- 1/8 teaspoon ground cloves
- 1 (1-pound) sirloin steak, cut in
- 1″ cubes
- 2 red bell peppers, cut in strips
- 2 green bell peppers, cut in strips

Directions:

1. In small bowl, combine brown sugar, garlic powder, cayenne pepper, onion salt, chili powder, and clove, and mix well. Toss sirloin steak with brown sugar mixture. Place in glass dish and cover; refrigerate for 2 hours.
2. When ready to cook, prepare and preheat grill. Thread steak cubes and pepper strips on metal skewers. Grill 6″ from medium coals for 5–8 minutes, turning once, until steak reaches desired doneness and peppers are crisp-tender. Serve immediately.

Nutrition Info:

- Info Per Serving: Calories: 205.53; Fat: 6.23 g ;Saturated fat: 2.24 g ;Sodium: 133.03 mg

Beef-risotto–stuffed Peppers

Servings: 4
Cooking Time: X
Ingredients:

- 1 tablespoon olive oil
- 1 onion, chopped
- 2 cups Beef Risotto
- 1 egg
- 1 egg white
- 1 tomato, chopped
- 2 slices Whole-Grain Oatmeal Bread
- 4 bell peppers
- 1 cup Spaghetti Sauce
- ¼ cup water

Directions:

1. Preheat oven to 350ºF. Spray a 9″-square baking pan with nonstick cooking spray and set aside. In medium saucepan, heat olive oil over medium heat. Add onion; cook and stir until tender, about 5 minutes. Remove from heat and stir in risotto, egg, egg white, and tomato and mix well.
2. Make crumbs from the bread and add to the risotto mixture. Cut off the pepper tops and remove membranes and seeds. Stuff with risotto mixture.
3. Place stuffed peppers in prepared baking dish. In small bowl, combine Spaghetti Sauce and water; pour over and around peppers. Cover with foil and bake for 45–55 minutes or until peppers are tender. Serve immediately.

Nutrition Info:

- Info Per Serving: Calories: 331.74; Fat:12.15 g ;Saturated fat:3.20g ;Sodium:130.25 mg

Grilled Coffee-rubbed Sirloin Steak

Servings: X
Cooking Time: 15 Minutes
Ingredients:
- 1 tablespoon espresso coffee powder
- 1½ teaspoons dark brown sugar
- 1 teaspoon smoky paprika
- ½ teaspoon chili powder
- ¼ teaspoon garlic powder
- ¼ teaspoon ground black pepper
- ¼ teaspoon salt
- 1 (10-ounce) sirloin steak, trimmed to ⅛-inch fat

Directions:
1. In a small bowl, stir together the espresso powder, sugar, paprika, chili powder, garlic powder, pepper, and salt.
2. Rub the coffee mixture all over the steak.
3. Preheat the grill to medium-high.
4. Grill the steak, turning once, until it is the desired doneness, about 7 minutes per side for medium (160°F).
5. Transfer the steak to a cutting board and let rest for at least 10 minutes before slicing it against the grain.
6. Serve.

Nutrition Info:
- Info Per Serving: Calories: 285 ; Fat: 18 g ;Saturated fat: 7 g ;Sodium: 274 mg

Dark Beer Beef Chili

Servings: X
Cooking Time: 50 Minutes
Ingredients:
- 1 teaspoon olive oil
- 6 ounces extra-lean ground beef
- ½ sweet onion, chopped
- 1 green bell pepper, diced
- 1 teaspoon minced garlic
- 2 cups low-sodium canned diced tomatoes, with their juices
- ½ cup low-sodium canned kidney beans, rinsed and drained
- ½ cup low-sodium canned lentils, rinsed and drained
- ½ cup dark beer
- 1 tablespoon chili powder
- ½ teaspoon ground cumin
- Pinch cayenne powder
- 2 teaspoons chopped fresh cilantro, for garnish
- 4 tablespoons fat-free sour cream, for garnish

Directions:
1. In a large saucepan, warm the oil over medium-high heat.
2. Add the ground beef and cook until browned, about 5 minutes.
3. Add the onions, bell pepper, and garlic and sauté until softened, about 4 minutes.
4. Stir in the tomatoes, kidney beans, lentils, beer, chili powder, cumin, and cayenne powder.
5. Bring the mixture to a boil and then reduce the heat. Simmer, partially covered, until the flavors come together and the liquid is almost gone, 35 to 40 minutes.
6. Serve topped with cilantro and sour cream.

Nutrition Info:
- Info Per Serving: Calories: 415 ; Fat: 10 g ;Saturated fat: 2 g ;Sodium: 125 mg

Wasabi-roasted Filet Mignon

Servings: 12
Cooking Time: X
Ingredients:

- 1 (3-pound) filet mignon roast
- ¼ teaspoon pepper
- 1 teaspoon powdered wasabi
- 2 tablespoons sesame oil
- 2 tablespoons soy sauce

Directions:

1. Preheat oven to 400ºF. If the roast has a thin end and a thick end, fold the thin end under so the roast is about the same thickness. Place on roasting pan.
2. In small bowl, combine pepper, wasabi, oil, and soy sauce, and mix well. Brush half over roast. Roast the beef for 30 minutes, then remove and brush with remaining wasabi mixture. Return to oven for 5–10 minutes longer or until meat thermometer registers at least 145ºF for medium rare.
3. Remove from oven, cover, and let stand for 15 minutes before slicing to serve.

Nutrition Info:

- Info Per Serving: Calories:298.15; Fat: 24.00g ;Saturated fat:8.99 g ;Sodium: 143.07 mg

Whole-grain Sausage Pizza

Servings: 6–8
Cooking Time: X
Ingredients:

- 8 ounces pork sausage
- 1 onion, chopped
- 1 (8-ounce) package sliced mushrooms
- 1 green bell pepper, chopped
- 1 (8-ounce) can low-sodium tomato sauce
- 2 tomatoes, chopped
- 1 teaspoon dried Italian seasoning
- 1 Whole-Grain Pizza Crust , prebaked
- 1 cup shredded part-skim mozzarella cheese
- 3 tablespoons grated Parmesan cheese

Directions:

1. Preheat oven to 400ºF. Crumble pork sausage into saucepan and place over medium heat. Cook until sausage is browned, stirring frequently. Remove pork from saucepan and drain excess fat, but do not wipe saucepan.
2. Add onion, mushrooms, and bell pepper to saucepan; cook, stirring to loosen drippings, for 3–4 minutes or until crisp-tender. Add tomato sauce, tomatoes, dried Italian seasoning, and pork sausage; cook and stir for 2 minutes.
3. Place pizza crust on cookie sheet and top with pork mixture. Sprinkle with cheeses. Bake for 20–25 minutes or until pizza is hot and cheese is melted and beginning to brown. Let stand for 5 minutes, then serve.

Nutrition Info:

- Info Per Serving: Calories:325.25 ; Fat:11.91 g ;Saturated fat: 4.17 g ;Sodium:349.87 mg

Pork Chops With Cabbage

Servings: 6
Cooking Time: X
Ingredients:
- 1 red onion, chopped
- 4 cloves garlic, minced
- 3 cups chopped red cabbage
- 3 cups chopped green cabbage
- 1 apple, chopped
- 6 (3-ounce) boneless pork chops
- 1/8 teaspoon white pepper
- 1 tablespoon olive oil
- ¼ cup brown sugar
- ¼ cup apple cider vinegar
- 1 tablespoon mustard

Directions:
1. In 4- to 5-quart slow cooker, combine onion, garlic, cabbages, and apple and mix well.
2. Trim pork chops of any excess fat and sprinkle with pepper. Heat olive oil in large saucepan over medium heat. Brown chops on just one side, about 3 minutes. Add to slow cooker with vegetables.
3. In small bowl, combine brown sugar, vinegar, and mustard and mix well. Pour into slow cooker. Cover and cook on low for 7–8 hours or until pork and cabbage are tender. Serve immediately.

Nutrition Info:
- Info Per Serving: Calories: 242.86 ; Fat: 10.57 g ;Saturated fat:3.37 g ;Sodium:364.80 mg

Skillet Beef Macaroni

Servings: X
Cooking Time: 20 Minutes
Ingredients:
- 2 teaspoons olive oil
- 6 ounces extra-lean ground beef
- 2 celery stalks, chopped
- ½ cup chopped sweet onion
- 1 teaspoon minced garlic
- 1 cup Double Tomato Sauce or your favorite low-sodium marinara sauce
- 1 tablespoon tomato paste
- 1 teaspoon chopped fresh oregano
- 1 teaspoon chopped fresh basil
- Pinch red pepper flakes
- 2 cups cooked whole-grain elbow pasta

Directions:
1. In a large skillet, warm the oil over medium-high heat.
2. Add the ground beef and cook until browned, about 6 minutes.
3. Add the celery, onions, and garlic and sauté until softened, about 4 minutes.
4. Stir in the tomato sauce, tomato paste, oregano, basil, and red pepper flakes and bring the sauce to a boil.
5. Reduce the heat to low and simmer the sauce for 10 minutes to allow the flavors to meld.
6. Stir in the pasta and serve.

Nutrition Info:
- Info Per Serving: Calories: 377; Fat: 10 g ;Saturated fat: 2 g ;Sodium: 312 mg

Fiery Pork Stir-fry

Servings: X
Cooking Time: 20 Minutes
Ingredients:

- For the sauce
- ¼ cup low-sodium chicken broth
- 1 tablespoon low-sodium tamari sauce
- 1 tablespoon honey
- 1 teaspoon cornstarch
- 1 teaspoon rice vinegar
- 1 teaspoon peeled, grated ginger
- ½ teaspoon minced garlic
- ⅛ teaspoon red pepper flakes
- For the stir-fry
- 2 teaspoons sesame oil
- 1 (8-ounce) pork tenderloin, cut into ¼-inch slices
- 1 carrot, thinly sliced
- 1 red bell pepper, thinly sliced
- 1 cup sliced mushrooms
- 1 cup small broccoli florets
- 1 cup green beans, cut into 1-inch pieces
- 1 scallion, green part only, thinly sliced, for garnish
- 2 tablespoons chopped cashews, for garnish

Directions:
1. To make the sauce
2. In a small bowl, stir together the chicken broth, tamari, honey, cornstarch, vinegar, ginger, garlic, and red pepper flakes.
3. Set aside.
4. To make the stir-fry
5. In a large skillet, warm the sesame oil over medium-high heat.
6. Add the pork and sauté until it is just cooked through, about 12 minutes.
7. Stir in the carrots, bell pepper, and mushrooms and stir-fry until the vegetables are tender, about 5 minutes.
8. Stir in the broccoli and green beans and stir-fry until the veggies are tender, about 4 minutes.
9. Add the sauce to the skillet and cook until the sauce thickens, about 3 minutes.
10. Stir to coat and serve topped with the scallions and cashews.

Nutrition Info:
- Info Per Serving: Calories: 321 ; Fat: 11 g ;Saturated fat: 2 g ;Sodium: 356 mg

Bbq Pork Chops

Servings: 8
Cooking Time: X
Ingredients:

- 2 tablespoons olive oil
- 1 onion, chopped
- 4 cloves garlic, minced
- 1 (14-ounce) can no-salt crushed tomatoes, undrained
- 1 cup low-sodium chili sauce
- 1 tablespoon lemon juice
- 2 tablespoons mustard
- ¼ cup brown sugar
- 2 tablespoons molasses
- ½ teaspoon cumin
- 1 teaspoon dried thyme leaves
- 1/8 teaspoon ground cloves
- 8 (3-ounce) boneless pork chops

Directions:
1. In large pot, heat olive oil over medium heat. Add onion and garlic; cook and stir for 3–4 minutes until crisp-tender. Add tomatoes, chili sauce, lemon juice, mustard, sugar, molasses, cumin, thyme, and cloves. Bring to a simmer, then reduce heat, cover, and simmer for 2 hours.
2. When ready to cook, prepare and preheat grill. Spray grill rack with nonstick cooking spray and add pork chops. Grill until the chops can be easily moved, about 4 minutes. Turn and brush with sauce. Cook for 3–5 minutes longer or until chops are just pink, turning again and brushing with more sauce. Serve with sauce that hasn't been used to brush the pork.

Nutrition Info:
- Info Per Serving: Calories:276.23 ; Fat:11.80 g ;Saturated fat: 3.53 g ;Sodium: 417.98 mg

Fish And Seafood

Salmon With Spicy Mixed Beans

Servings: 4
Cooking Time: 20 Minutes
Ingredients:

- 2 teaspoons olive oil, divided
- 4 (4-ounce) salmon fillets
- Pinch salt
- ⅛ teaspoon black pepper
- 1 onion, diced
- 3 cloves peeled garlic, minced
- 1 jalapeño pepper, seeded and minced
- 1 (16-ounce) can low-sodium mixed beans, rinsed and drained
- 2 tablespoons low-fat plain Greek yogurt
- 2 tablespoons minced fresh cilantro

Directions:
1. Put 1 teaspoon of the olive oil in a large skillet and heat over medium heat.
2. Sprinkle the salmon fillets with the salt and pepper and add to the skillet, skin side down.
3. Cook for 5 minutes, then flip the fillets with a spatula and cook for another 3 to 4 minutes or until the salmon flakes when tested with a fork. Remove the fish to a clean warm plate, and cover with an aluminum foil tent to keep warm.
4. Add the remaining 1 teaspoon of the olive oil to the skillet. Add the onion, garlic, and jalapeño pepper; cook, stirring frequently, for 3 minutes.
5. Add the beans and mash with a fork until desired consistency.
6. Remove the pan from the heat, add the yogurt, and stir until combined.
7. Pile the beans onto a serving platter, top with the fish, and sprinkle with the cilantro. Serve immediately.

Nutrition Info:
- Info Per Serving: Calories: 293 ; Fat: 10 g ;Saturated fat: 2 g;Sodium: 345 mg

Salmon Vegetable Stir-fry

Servings: 4
Cooking Time: X
Ingredients:

- 2 tablespoons rice vinegar
- 1 tablespoon sugar
- 1 tablespoon grated ginger root
- 1 tablespoon cornstarch
- 2 tablespoons hoisin sauce
- 1/8 teaspoon white pepper
- 2 tablespoons peanut oil
- 1 onion, sliced
- ½ pound sugar-snap peas
- 3 carrots, sliced
- 1 red bell pepper, sliced
- ¼ pound salmon fillet

Directions:
1. In small bowl, combine rice vinegar, sugar, ginger root, cornstarch, hoi-sin sauce, and pepper. Mix well and set aside.
2. In large skillet or wok, heat peanut oil over high heat. Add onion, peas, and carrots. Stir-fry for 3–4 minutes or until vegetables begin to soften. Add red bell pepper.
3. Immediately place salmon fillet on top of vegetables. Reduce heat to medium, cover skillet or wok and cook for 4–5 minutes or until salmon flakes when tested with fork.
4. Stir the vinegar mixture and add to skillet or wok. Turn heat to medium-high and stir-fry to break up the salmon for 2–3 minutes until the sauce bubbles and thickens. Serve immediately over hot cooked rice.

Nutrition Info:
- Info Per Serving: Calories: 371.71; Fat:11.73 g ;Saturated fat: 3.24 g ;Sodium: 237.60 mg

Poached Fish With Tomatoes And Capers

Servings: 4
Cooking Time: X
Ingredients:

- 2 tablespoons olive oil
- ½ cup chopped red onion
- 2 cloves garlic, minced
- 1 cup chopped fresh tomatoes
- 2 tablespoons no-salt tomato paste
- ¼ cup dry white wine
- 2 tablespoons capers, rinsed
- 4 (4-ounce) white fish fillets
- ¼ cup chopped parsley

Directions:

1. In large skillet, heat olive oil over medium heat. Add onion and garlic; cook and stir until tender, about 5 minutes. Add tomatoes, tomato paste, and wine and bring to a simmer; simmer for 5 minutes, stirring frequently.
2. Add capers to sauce and stir, then arrange fillets on top of sauce. Spoon sauce over fish. Reduce heat to low, cover, and poach for 7–10 minutes, or until fish flakes when tested with fork. Sprinkle with parsley and serve immediately.

Nutrition Info:

- Info Per Serving: Calories: 191.05 ; Fat:7.70 g ;Saturated fat: 1.13 g ;Sodium: 199.73 mg

Mediterranean Roasted Mahi Mahi With Broccoli

Servings: 4
Cooking Time: 22 Minutes
Ingredients:

- 2 cups broccoli florets
- 2 tablespoons olive oil, divided
- 4 (6-ounce) mahi mahi fillets
- 1 cup cherry tomatoes
- 2 cloves peeled garlic, sliced
- ⅛ teaspoon white pepper
- 1 teaspoon paprika
- 2 tablespoons fresh lemon juice
- 2 tablespoons crumbled feta cheese

Directions:

1. Preheat the oven to 400°F. Line a baking sheet with parchment paper.
2. Place the broccoli florets on the prepared baking sheet. Drizzle with 1 tablespoon of the olive oil and toss to coat. Spread the broccoli in a single layer.
3. Roast the broccoli for 10 minutes.
4. Remove the baking sheet from the oven. Move the broccoli over to make room for the fish. Place the fish, cherry tomatoes, and garlic on the baking sheet. Sprinkle the fish with the white pepper and paprika.
5. In a small bowl, combine the lemon juice and the remaining 1 tablespoon olive oil, and drizzle over the fish and vegetable mixture.
6. Roast for 10 to 12 minutes longer, or until the fish flakes when tested with a fork and the broccoli is tender.
7. Sprinkle with the feta cheese and serve immediately.

Nutrition Info:

- Info Per Serving: Calories: 258; Fat: 11 g ;Saturated fat: 2 g;Sodium: 171 mg

Roasted Shrimp And Veggies

Servings: 4
Cooking Time: 20 Minutes
Ingredients:
- 1 cup sliced cremini mushrooms
- 2 medium chopped Yukon Gold potatoes, rinsed, unpeeled
- 2 cups broccoli florets
- 3 cloves garlic, sliced
- 1 cup sliced fresh green beans
- 1 cup cauliflower florets
- 2 tablespoons fresh lemon juice
- 2 tablespoons low-sodium vegetable broth
- 1 teaspoon olive oil
- 1 teaspoon dried thyme
- ½ teaspoon dried oregano
- Pinch salt
- ⅛ teaspoon black pepper
- ½ pound medium shrimp, peeled and deveined

Directions:
1. Preheat the oven to 400°F.
2. In a large baking pan, combine the mushrooms, potatoes, broccoli, garlic, green beans, and cauliflower, and toss to coat.
3. In a small bowl, combine the lemon juice, broth, olive oil, thyme, oregano, salt, and pepper and mix well. Drizzle over the vegetables
4. Roast for 15 minutes, then stir.
5. Add the shrimp and distribute evenly.
6. Roast for another 5 minutes or until the shrimp curl and turn pink. Serve immediately.

Nutrition Info:
- Info Per Serving: Calories:192 ; Fat: 3 g ;Saturated fat: 0 g;Sodium: 116 mg

Salmon With Farro Pilaf

Servings: 4
Cooking Time: 25 Minutes
Ingredients:
- ½ cup farro
- 1¼ cups low-sodium vegetable broth
- 4 (4-ounce) salmon fillets
- Pinch salt
- ½ teaspoon dried marjoram leaves
- ⅛ teaspoon white pepper
- ¼ cup dried cherries
- ¼ cup dried currants
- 1 cup fresh baby spinach leaves
- 1 tablespoon orange juice

Directions:
1. Preheat the oven to 400°F. Line a baking sheet with parchment paper and set aside.
2. In a medium saucepan over medium heat, combine the farro and the vegetable broth and bring to a simmer. Reduce the heat to low and simmer, partially covered, for 25 minutes, or until the farro is tender.
3. Meanwhile, sprinkle the salmon with the salt, marjoram, and white pepper and place on the prepared baking sheet.
4. When the farro has cooked for 10 minutes, bake the salmon in the oven for 12 to 15 minutes, or until the salmon flakes when tested with a fork. Remove and cover to keep warm.
5. When the farro is tender, add the cherries, currants, spinach, and orange juice; stir and cover. Let stand off the heat for 2 to 3 minutes.
6. Plate the salmon and serve with the farro pilaf.

Nutrition Info:
- Info Per Serving: Calories: 304 ; Fat: 8 g ;Saturated fat: 2 g;Sodium: 139 mg

Fennel-grilled Haddock

Servings: 4
Cooking Time: X
Ingredients:

- 2 bulbs fennel
- 4 (5-ounce) haddock or halibut steaks
- 3 tablespoons olive oil Pinch salt
- 1/8 teaspoon cayenne pepper
- 1 teaspoon paprika
- 2 tablespoons lemon juice

Directions:

1. Prepare and preheat grill. Slice fennel bulbs lengthwise into ½" slices, leaving the stalks and fronds attached.
2. Brush fennel and haddock with olive oil on all sides to coat. Sprinkle fish with salt, pepper, and paprika. Place fennel on grill 6″ above medium coals, cut side down. Arrange fish on top of fennel and close the grill.
3. Grill for 5–7 minutes or until fennel is deep golden brown and fish flakes when tested with fork. Remove fish to serving platter, sprinkle with lemon juice, and cover.
4. Cut the root end and stems from the fennel and discard. Slice fennel and place on top of fish; serve immediately.

Nutrition Info:

- Info Per Serving: Calories: 246.68; Fat: 11.35 g ;Saturated fat:1.58 g ;Sodium: 192.31 mg

Almond Snapper With Shrimp Sauce

Servings: 6
Cooking Time: X
Ingredients:

- 1 egg white
- ¼ cup dry breadcrumbs
- 1/3 cup ground almonds
- 1/8 teaspoon salt
- 1/8 teaspoon white pepper
- 6 (4-ounce) red snapper fillets
- 3 tablespoons olive oil, divided
- 1 onion, chopped
- 4 cloves garlic, minced
- 1 red bell pepper, chopped
- ¼ pound small raw shrimp
- 1 tablespoon lemon juice
- ½ cup low-fat sour cream
- ½ teaspoon dried dill weed

Directions:

1. Place egg white in shallow bowl; beat until foamy. On shallow plate, combine breadcrumbs, almonds, salt, and pepper and mix well. Dip fish into egg white, then into crumb mixture, pressing to coat. Let stand on wire rack for 10 minutes.
2. In small saucepan, heat 1 tablespoon olive oil over medium heat. Add onion, garlic, and bell pepper; cook and stir until tender, about 5 minutes. Add shrimp; cook and stir just until shrimp curl and turn pink, about 1–2 minutes. Remove from heat and add lemon juice; set aside.
3. In large saucepan, heat remaining 2 tablespoons olive oil over medium heat. Add coated fish fillets. Cook for 4 minutes on one side, then carefully turn and cook for 2–5 minutes on second side until coating is browned and fish flakes when tested with a fork.
4. While fish is cooking, return saucepan with shrimp to medium heat. Add sour cream and dill weed. Heat, stirring, until mixture is hot.
5. Remove fish from skillet and place on serving plate. Top each with a spoonful of shrimp sauce and serve immediately.

Nutrition Info:

- Info Per Serving: Calories:272.57 ; Fat:13.80 g ;Saturated fat: 3.09 g;Sodium:216.17 mg

Fried Mahi-mahi

Servings: 4
Cooking Time: 20 Min
Ingredients:
- 1 lb. mahi-mahi fillets
- ½ tsp fine sea salt
- ¼ tsp ground black pepper
- 1 tbsp. olive oil
- 1 medium green bell pepper, cored and chopped
- 1 small brown onion, chopped
- 2 cups grape tomatoes
- ¼ cup black olives, pitted and chopped

Directions:
1. Season the mahi-mahi fillets with salt and pepper.
2. Heat the olive oil in a large nonstick frying pan over medium-high heat.
3. Add the green bell pepper and onion. Cook for 3 to 5 minutes, until softened.
4. Add the grape tomatoes and black olives. Mix for 1 to 2 minutes, until the tomatoes have softened.
5. Place the mahi-mahi fillets on top of the vegetables and cover with a lid. Cook for 5 to 10 minutes, or until the fish flakes with a fork. Remove from the heat and serve.

Nutrition Info:
- Info Per Serving: Calories: 151 ; Fat: 5 g ;Saturated fat: 1 g ;Sodium: 603 mg

Cod Satay

Servings: 4
Cooking Time: 15 Minutes
Ingredients:
- 2 teaspoons olive oil, divided
- 1 small onion, diced
- 2 cloves garlic, minced
- ⅓ cup low-fat coconut milk
- 1 tomato, chopped
- 2 tablespoons low-fat peanut butter
- 1 tablespoon packed brown sugar
- ⅓ cup low-sodium vegetable broth
- 2 teaspoons low-sodium soy sauce
- ⅛ teaspoon ground ginger
- Pinch red pepper flakes
- 4 (6-ounce) cod fillets
- ⅛ teaspoon white pepper

Directions:
1. In a small saucepan, heat 1 teaspoon of the olive oil over medium heat.
2. Add the onion and garlic, and cook, stirring frequently for 3 minutes.
3. Add the coconut milk, tomato, peanut butter, brown sugar, broth, soy sauce, ginger, and red pepper flakes, and bring to a simmer, stirring with a whisk until the sauce combines. Simmer for 2 minutes, then remove the satay sauce from the heat and set aside.
4. Season the cod with the white pepper.
5. Heat a large nonstick skillet with the remaining 1 teaspoon olive oil, and add the cod fillets. Cook for 3 minutes, then turn and cook for 3 to 4 minutes more or until the fish flakes when tested with a fork.
6. Cover the fish with the satay sauce and serve immediately.

Nutrition Info:
- Info Per Serving: Calories: 255 ; Fat: 10 g ;Saturated fat: 5 g;Sodium: 222 mg

Northwest Salmon

Servings: 4
Cooking Time: X
Ingredients:

- 4 tablespoons olive oil, divided
- 5 juniper berries, crushed
- ½ cup chopped red onion
- 1 cup blueberries
- ½ cup chopped hazelnuts
- ¼ cup dry white wine
- 4 (5-ounce) salmon fillets Pinch salt
- 1/8 teaspoon white pepper
- 2 cups watercress

Directions:

1. Preheat grill or broiler. In small saucepan, heat 3 tablespoons of the olive oil. Add juniper berries and red onion; cook and stir for 3 minutes. Add blueberries, hazelnuts, and wine and bring to a simmer.
2. Meanwhile, sprinkle salmon with salt and pepper and brush with olive oil. Broil or grill 6″ from heat until salmon flakes when tested with a fork. Place salmon on watercress and pour blueberry sauce over all; serve immediately.

Nutrition Info:

- Info Per Serving: Calories: 362.66; Fat:22.63 g ;Saturated fat:3.27 g ;Sodium: 105.81 mg

Tuna Patties

Servings: 6
Cooking Time: 10 Min
Ingredients:

- 12 oz canned, water-packed tuna, drained
- 4 tbsp. almond flour
- 1 large free-range egg white
- 1 tbsp. brown onion, finely chopped
- ½ lemon, juiced
- ½ tsp parsley, finely chopped
- Pinch red pepper flakes
- Pinch Himalayan pink salt
- Pinch ground black pepper
- Cooking spray

Directions:

1. In a medium-sized mixing bowl, add the tuna, almond flour, egg white, onions, lemon juice, parsley, red pepper flakes, salt, and pepper, mix to combine.
2. Mold the tuna mixture into 6 equal patties.
3. Place the tuna cakes on a plate and chill for 1 hour in the refrigerator until firm.
4. Spray a large, heavy-bottom pan with cooking spray and place it over medium-high heat.
5. Add the tuna cakes to the pan and cook for 5 minutes per side, turning once, until browned and heated through. Serve.

Nutrition Info:

- Info Per Serving: Calories: 243 ; Fat: 6 g ;Saturated fat: 0 g ;Sodium: 558 mg

Baked Lemon Sole With Herbed Crumbs

Servings: 4
Cooking Time: X
Ingredients:

- 2 slices Light Whole-Grain Bread , crumbled
- 2 tablespoons minced parsley
- 2 cloves garlic, minced
- 1 teaspoon dried dill weed
- 2 tablespoons olive oil
- 4 (6-ounce) sole fillets
- 2 tablespoons lemon juice Pinch salt
- 1/8 teaspoon white pepper

Directions:

1. Preheat oven to 350ºF. In small bowl, combine breadcrumbs, parsley, garlic, and dill weed, and mix well. Drizzle with olive oil and toss to coat.
2. Spray a 9″ baking dish with nonstick cooking spray and arrange fillets in dish. Sprinkle with lemon juice, salt, and pepper. Divide crumb mixture on top of fillets.
3. Bake for 12–17 minutes or until fish flakes when tested with a fork and crumb topping is browned. Serve immediately.

Nutrition Info:

- Info Per Serving: Calories: 294.58; Fat:9.86 g ;Saturated fat:1.65 g ;Sodium:288.21 mg

Halibut Burgers

Servings: 4
Cooking Time: 35 Min
Ingredients:

- Aluminum foil
- 1 lb. halibut fillets
- ½ tsp Himalayan pink salt, divided
- ¼ tsp ground black pepper
- ½ cup whole wheat breadcrumbs
- 1 large free-range egg
- 1 tbsp. garlic, crushed
- ½ tsp dried dill
- 2 tbsp. avocado oil
- 4 whole wheat buns

Directions:

1. Heat the oven to 400°F gas mark 6. Line a baking sheet with aluminum foil.
2. Place the halibut fillets on the baking sheet and season with ¼ tsp salt and pepper. Bake for 15 to 20 minutes, or until the halibut flakes with a fork. Remove from the oven.
3. Transfer the flesh into a medium-sized mixing bowl, removing any bones.
4. Add the breadcrumbs, egg, garlic, dill and the remaining ¼ tsp salt, mix to combine.
5. Mold the fish mixture into 4 patties.
6. Heat the avocado oil in a large heavy bottom pan over medium heat.
7. Gently place the halibut patties in the pan. Fry for 5 to 6 minutes, until browned, flip, and cook for 3 to 5 minutes, remove from the heat.
8. Place 1 fish patty on each of the 4 buns and serve.

Nutrition Info:

- Info Per Serving: Calories: 294 ; Fat: 16 g ;Saturated fat: 3 g ;Sodium: 458 mg

Orange Thyme Red Snapper

Servings: 4
Cooking Time: 10 Minutes
Ingredients:
- 1 medium orange
- 2 teaspoons olive oil
- 4 (6-ounce) fillets red snapper
- Pinch salt
- ⅛ teaspoon white pepper
- 2 teaspoons olive oil
- 2 scallions, chopped
- 1½ teaspoons fresh thyme leaves, or ½ teaspoon dried

Directions:
1. Rinse the orange and dry. Using a small grater or zester, remove 1 teaspoon zest from the orange and set aside. Cut the orange in half, squeeze in a small bowl, and reserve the juice.
2. Add the olive oil to a large nonstick skillet and place over medium heat. Meanwhile, sprinkle the fish with the salt and white pepper.
3. Add the fish to the skillet, skin-side down, if the skin is attached. Cook 3 minutes on one side, briefly pressing on the fish with a spatula to prevent curling (or slit the fillet to prevent curling). Turn the fish and cook for 2 to 3 minutes on the second side, until the fish flakes when tested with a fork.
4. Transfer the fish to a plate. Remove the skin, if present, and discard. Cover the fish with a foil tent to keep it warm.
5. Add the scallions and the thyme to the skillet; cook and stir gently for 1 minute. Add the reserved orange juice and orange zest and simmer for 2 to 3 minutes or until the liquid is slightly reduced.
6. Pour the sauce over the fish and serve immediately.

Nutrition Info:
- Info Per Serving: Calories: 232 ; Fat: 7 g ;Saturated fat: 1 g;Sodium: 121 mg

Sesame-crusted Mahi Mahi

Servings: 4
Cooking Time: X
Ingredients:
- 4 (4-ounce) mahi mahi or sole fillets
- 2 tablespoons Dijon mustard
- 1 tablespoon low-fat sour cream
- ½ cup sesame seeds
- 2 tablespoons olive oil
- 1 lemon, cut into wedges

Directions:
1. Rinse fillets and pat dry. In small bowl, combine mustard and sour cream and mix well. Spread this mixture on all sides of fish. Roll in sesame seeds to coat.
2. Heat olive oil in large skillet over medium heat. Pan-fry fish, turning once, for 5–8 minutes or until fish flakes when tested with fork and sesame seeds are toasted. Serve immediately with lemon wedges.

Nutrition Info:
- Info Per Serving: Calories: 282.75; Fat: 17.17 g ;Saturated fat:2.84 g ;Sodium: 209.54 mg

Shrimp Stir-fry

Servings: 2
Cooking Time: 15 Min
Ingredients:

- 12 oz zucchini spirals
- 2 tsp low-sodium tamari sauce
- 2 tsp apple cider vinegar
- 1 tsp ginger, peeled and grated
- 1 tsp garlic, crushed
- 1 tsp organic honey
- 2 tsp sesame oil
- 6 oz shrimp, peeled and deveined
- 2 cups napa cabbage, shredded
- 1 medium green bell pepper, thinly sliced
- 1 spring onion, thinly sliced
- 1 tbsp. toasted sesame seeds, for garnish

Directions:
1. Cook the zucchini according to the package directions. Drain and run under cold water to stop the cooking process. Transfer the zucchini to a medium-sized mixing bowl and set aside.
2. In a small-sized mixing bowl, add the tamari sauce, apple cider vinegar, ginger, garlic, and honey, mix to combine, and set aside.
3. Warm the sesame oil in a medium-sized, heavy-bottom pan over medium-high heat. Add the shrimp and fry for 5 minutes until cooked through.
4. Add the napa cabbage, green bell pepper, and spring onion and fry for 4 minutes until the vegetables are tender. Add the tamari sauce mixture and the zucchini, toss to coat, heat for 1 minute.
5. Serve into bowls and top with sesame seeds.

Nutrition Info:
- Info Per Serving: Calories: 400 ; Fat: 8 g ;Saturated fat: 1 g ;Sodium: 347 mg

Citrus Cod Bake

Servings: 2
Cooking Time: 25 Min
Ingredients:

- 2 tbsp. garlic, crushed
- 1 tbsp. olive oil
- 2 rosemary sprigs, stem removed and finely chopped
- 2 oregano sprigs, finely chopped
- 2 cod fillets, rinsed and patted dry
- ¼ tsp Himalayan pink salt
- ¼ tsp ground black pepper
- 1 lime, cut into 4 round slices
- ½ lemon, wedged

Directions:
1. Heat the oven to 450°F gas mark 8.
2. In a small-sized mixing bowl, add the garlic, olive oil, rosemary, and oregano, mix to combine.
3. Place the cod fillets on a baking sheet and season with salt and pepper.
4. Evenly coat both cod fillets with the garlic and herb mixture. Place 2 lime slices on each fillet. Bake for 18 to 25 minutes, or until the cod fillets are completely cooked.
5. Serve with a lemon wedge.

Nutrition Info:
- Info Per Serving: Calories: 218 ; Fat:3 g ;Saturated fat: 1 g ;Sodium: 430 mg

Catalán Salmon Tacos

Servings: 4
Cooking Time: 20 Minutes
Ingredients:
- 1 teaspoon olive oil
- 1 (6-ounce) salmon fillet
- 1 teaspoon chili powder
- ½ teaspoon dried oregano leaves
- ⅛ teaspoon black pepper
- 1 small onion, diced
- 2 cloves peeled garlic, minced
- 1 (16-ounce) can low-sodium white beans, rinsed and drained
- 1 tomato, chopped
- 1 cup torn fresh Swiss chard leaves
- 2 tablespoons pine nuts
- 4 corn tortillas, heated

Directions:
1. Add the olive oil to a large nonstick skillet and place over medium heat. Rub the salmon fillet with the chili powder, oregano, and pepper.
2. Add the salmon to the pan, skin side down. Cook for 3 minutes, then turn and cook for 5 minutes longer, or until the fish flakes when tested with a fork. Remove the salmon from the pan, flake, and set aside.
3. Add the onion and garlic to the pan and cook for 2 to 3 minutes, stirring frequently, until softened.
4. Add the beans and mash some of them into the onions. Cook for 1 minute, stirring occasionally.
5. Add the tomato and Swiss chard and cook for another 1 to 2 minutes until the greens start to wilt. Add the pine nuts to the mixture.
6. Make the tacos by adding the bean mixture and the salmon to the corn tortillas, and fold them in half. Serve immediately.

Nutrition Info:
- Info Per Serving: Calories: 296 ; Fat: 8 g ;Saturated fat: 1 g;Sodium: 63 mg

Poached Chilean Sea Bass With Pears

Servings: 4
Cooking Time: X
Ingredients:
- ½ cup dry white wine
- ¼ cup water
- 2 bay leaves
- 1/8 teaspoon salt
- ½ teaspoon Tabasco sauce
- 1 lemon, thinly sliced
- 4 (4–5) ounce sea bass steaks or fillets
- 2 firm pears, cored and cut in half
- 1 tablespoon butter

Directions:
1. In large skillet, combine wine, water, bay leaves, salt, Tabasco, and lemon slices. Bring to a simmer over medium heat.
2. Add fish and pears. Reduce heat to low and poach for 9–12 minutes or until fish flakes when tested with a fork.
3. Remove fish and pears to serving platter. Remove bay leaves from poaching liquid and increase heat to high. Boil for 3–5 minutes or until liquid is reduced and syrupy. Swirl in butter and pour over fish and pears; serve immediately.

Nutrition Info:
- Info Per Serving: Calories:235.38 ; Fat: 5.81 g ;Saturated fat: 2.55 g ;Sodium:194.06 mg

Healthy Paella

Servings: 4
Cooking Time: 15 Minutes
Ingredients:
- 1 tablespoon olive oil
- 1 onion, chopped
- 3 cloves garlic, minced
- 1 red bell pepper, seeded and chopped
- 2½ cups low-sodium vegetable broth
- 1 tomato, chopped
- 1 teaspoon smoked paprika
- 1 teaspoon dried thyme leaves
- ¼ teaspoon turmeric
- ⅛ teaspoon black pepper
- 1 cup whole-wheat orzo
- ½ pound halibut fillets, cut into 1-inch pieces
- 12 medium shrimp, peeled and deveined
- ¼ cup chopped fresh flat-leaf parsley

Directions:
1. In a large deep skillet, heat the olive oil over medium heat.
2. Add the onion, garlic, and red bell pepper, and cook, stirring, for 2 minutes.
3. Add the vegetable broth, tomato, paprika, thyme, turmeric, and black pepper, and bring to a simmer.
4. Stir in the orzo, making sure it is submerged in the liquid in the pan. Simmer for 5 minutes, stirring occasionally.
5. Add the halibut and stir. Simmer for 4 minutes.
6. Add the shrimp and stir. Simmer for 2 to 3 minutes or until the shrimp curl and turn pink and the pasta is cooked al dente.
7. Sprinkle with the parsley, and serve immediately.

Nutrition Info:
- Info Per Serving: Calories: 367 ; Fat: 7 g ;Saturated fat: 1 g;Sodium: 147 mg

Walnut Crusted Salmon

Servings: 4
Cooking Time: 20 Min
Ingredients:
- ¼ cup walnuts, chopped
- ¼ cup Parmesan cheese, finely shredded
- 2 tbsp. cilantro, chopped
- 1 tbsp. basil, chopped
- 1 lb. salmon fillets
- 2 tbsp. sesame oil
- ¼ tsp Himalayan pink salt
- ¼ tsp ground black pepper

Directions:
1. Heat the oven to 400°F gas mark 6.
2. In a food processor, add the walnuts and parmesan cheese. Process until it resembles fine crumbs.
3. Add the cilantro and basil, pulse until well combined.
4. Place the salmon fillets on a baking sheet and brush with sesame oil, season with salt and pepper.
5. Coat each oiled salmon fillet with the walnut and parmesan mixture. Bake for 15 to 20 minutes, or until the fillets have cooked through and the walnut mixture has browned. Remove from the oven and serve warm.

Nutrition Info:
- Info Per Serving: Calories: 244 ; Fat: 15 g ;Saturated fat: 3 g ;Sodium: 338 mg

Vegetarian Mains

Spaghetti Sauce

Servings: 6
Cooking Time: X
Ingredients:

- 2 tablespoons olive oil
- 1 onion, chopped
- 4 cloves garlic, minced
- 1 cup chopped celery
- 1 (8-ounce) package sliced mushrooms
- 1 (6-ounce) can no-salt tomato paste
- 2 (14-ounce) cans no-salt diced tomatoes, undrained
- 1 tablespoon dried Italian seasoning
- ½ cup grated carrots
- 1/8 teaspoon white pepper
- ½ cup dry red wine
- ½ cup water

Directions:

1. In large saucepan, heat olive oil over medium heat. Add onion and garlic; cook and stir until crisp-tender, about 4 minutes. Add celery and mushrooms; cook and stir for 2–3 minutes longer.
2. Add tomato paste; let paste brown a bit without stirring (this adds flavor to the sauce). Then add remaining ingredients and stir gently but thoroughly.
3. Bring sauce to a simmer, then reduce heat to low and partially cover. Simmer for 60–70 minutes, stirring occasionally, until sauce is blended and thickened. Serve over hot cooked pasta, couscous, or rice.

Nutrition Info:

- Info Per Serving: Calories: 155.73; Fat:5.11 g ;Saturated fat:0.72 g ;Sodium: 84.74 mg

Smoky Bean And Lentil Chili

Servings: X
Cooking Time: 30 Minutes
Ingredients:

- 1 teaspoon olive oil
- 1 red bell pepper, diced
- ¼ cup chopped sweet onion
- 1 teaspoon minced garlic
- 2 tablespoons chili powder
- 1 teaspoon smoked sweet paprika
- 1 cup low-sodium canned black beans, rinsed and drained
- 1 cup low-sodium canned lentils, rinsed and drained
- 1 cup shelled edamame
- 1 cup low-sodium canned diced tomatoes, drained
- ½ cup corn kernels
- ½ diced avocado, for garnish

Directions:

1. In a large saucepan, warm the olive oil over medium-high heat.
2. Add the bell pepper, onions, and garlic and sauté until softened, about 4 minutes. Stir in the chili powder and paprika and sauté 1 minute.
3. Stir in the black beans, lentils, edamame, tomatoes, and corn and lower the heat to medium. Cook, stirring occasionally, until the chili is hot and fragrant, about 25 minutes.
4. Serve topped with avocado.

Nutrition Info:

- Info Per Serving: Calories: 512 ; Fat: 16 g ;Saturated fat: 2 g ;Sodium: 105 mg

Peanut-butter-banana Skewered Sammies

Servings: 4–6
Cooking Time: X

Ingredients:

- ½ cup natural no-salt peanut butter
- 8 slices Honey-Wheat Sesame Bread
- 2 bananas
- 2 tablespoons lime juice
- 2 tablespoons butter or margarine, softened

Directions:

1. Spread peanut butter on one side of each slice of bread. Slice bananas, and as you work, sprinkle with lime juice. Make sandwiches by putting the bananas on the peanut butter and combining slices.
2. Butter the outsides of the sandwiches. Heat grill and cook sandwiches until bread is crisp and golden brown. Remove from grill, cut into quarters, and skewer on wood or metal skewers. Serve immediately.

Nutrition Info:

- Info Per Serving: Calories:376.36; Fat:18.67 g ;Saturated fat: 5.57 g ;Sodium: 77.44 mg

Hearty Vegetable Stew

Servings: X
Cooking Time: 25 Minutes

Ingredients:

- 2 teaspoons olive oil
- 2 celery stalks, chopped
- ½ sweet onion, peeled and chopped
- 1 teaspoon minced garlic
- 3 cups low-sodium vegetable broth
- 1 cup chopped tomatoes
- 2 carrots, thinly sliced
- 1 cup cauliflower florets
- 1 cup broccoli florets
- 1 yellow bell pepper, diced
- 1 cup low-sodium canned black beans, rinsed and drained
- Pinch red pepper flakes
- Sea salt
- Freshly ground black pepper
- 2 tablespoons grated low-fat Parmesan cheese, for garnish
- 1 tablespoon chopped fresh parsley, for garnish

Directions:

1. In a large saucepan, warm the olive oil over medium-high heat.
2. Add the celery, onions, and garlic and sauté until softened, about 4 minutes.
3. Stir in the vegetable broth, tomatoes, carrots, cauliflower, broccoli, bell peppers, black beans, and red pepper flakes.
4. Bring the stew to a boil, then reduce the heat to low and simmer until the vegetables are tender, 18 to 20 minutes.
5. Season with salt and pepper.
6. Serve topped with Parmesan cheese and parsley.

Nutrition Info:

- Info Per Serving: Calories:270 ; Fat: 8g ;Saturated fat: 3g ;Sodium: 237 mg

Baba Ghanoush With Fennel Stew

Servings: X
Cooking Time: 42 Minutes

Ingredients:

- 2 small eggplants, cut in half and scored with a crosshatch pattern on the cut sides
- 2 teaspoons olive oil
- 1 cup chopped fennel
- ½ cup chopped sweet onion
- 1 teaspoon minced garlic
- ½ teaspoon ground cumin
- ¼ teaspoon ground coriander
- 4 cups low-sodium vegetable broth
- 2 tablespoons tahini
- Juice of ½ lemon
- 2 tomatoes, chopped
- Sea salt
- Freshly ground black pepper
- 1 teaspoon chopped fresh parsley, for garnish

Directions:

1. Preheat the oven to 400°F.
2. Line a baking sheet with parchment paper and place the eggplant, cut-side down, on the sheet.
3. Roast the eggplant until soft and collapsed, 20 to 25 minutes. Remove from the oven and set aside to cool slightly for 10 minutes.
4. In a large saucepan, warm the olive oil over medium-high heat. Add the fennel, onion, garlic, cumin, and coriander and sauté until softened, 6 to 7 minutes.
5. Discarding the skin, place the roasted eggplant into a blender or food processor. Add the vegetable broth, tahini, and lemon juice and purée until smooth.
6. Add the puréed eggplant to the saucepan and stir in the tomatoes. Bring the mixture to a boil, then reduce the heat to low and simmer 10 minutes.
7. Season with salt and pepper.
8. Serve topped with parsley.

Nutrition Info:

- Info Per Serving: Calories: 338 ; Fat: 14 g ;Saturated fat: 2 g ;Sodium: 287 mg

Cannellini Bean–stuffed Sweet Potatoes

Servings: X
Cooking Time: 25 Minutes

Ingredients:

- 2 large sweet potatoes
- 1 teaspoon olive oil
- 1 cup low-sodium canned white cannellini beans, rinsed and drained
- 1 red bell pepper, chopped
- ½ cup chopped sweet onion
- 1 teaspoon minced garlic
- 1 cup shredded kale
- 1 tomato, chopped
- 1 teaspoon chopped fresh basil
- ½ teaspoon chopped fresh oregano
- Sea salt
- Freshly ground black pepper
- 2 tablespoons roasted pumpkin seeds, for garnish

Directions:

1. Preheat the oven to 350°F.
2. Pierce the sweet potatoes with a fork and place them in an 8-by-8-inch baking dish. Bake until tender, about 45 minutes.
3. While the potatoes are baking, warm the olive oil in a medium skillet over medium-high heat. Add the cannellini beans, bell peppers, onions, and garlic and sauté until heated through and tender, about 10 minutes.
4. Stir in the kale, tomatoes, basil, and oregano and sauté until the greens are wilted, about 3 minutes.
5. Season the bean mixture with salt and pepper.
6. Cut each baked potato in half lengthwise from end to end. Scoop out about half of the sweet potato flesh, reserving it for use in another meal or recipe. Spoon the bean mixture into the potatoes.
7. Serve topped with pumpkin seeds.

Nutrition Info:

- Info Per Serving: Calories: 406 ; Fat: 11 g ;Saturated fat: 2 g ;Sodium: 96 mg

Southwestern Millet-stuffed Tomatoes

Servings: X
Cooking Time: 25 Minutes
Ingredients:

- 4 large tomatoes
- ¼ teaspoon sea salt
- 2 teaspoon olive oil
- 1 sweet onion, chopped
- 1 orange bell pepper, chopped
- 2 small zucchini, chopped
- ½ jalapeño pepper, finely chopped
- 1 teaspoon minced garlic
- 2 cups cooked millet
- 1 cup fresh or frozen corn kernels (thawed, if frozen)
- Juice of ½ lime
- ¼ cup grated Parmesan cheese
- 2 teaspoons chopped fresh cilantro, for garnish

Directions:
1. Preheat the oven to 350°F.
2. Cut the tops off the tomatoes and discard. Carefully scoop out the insides of the tomatoes, leaving the shells intact. Sprinkle the inside of the tomatoes with salt and turn them upside down on paper towels to drain for about 15 minutes.
3. While the tomatoes are draining, warm the olive oil in a large skillet over medium-high heat.
4. Add the onions, bell peppers, zucchini, jalapeño, and garlic and sauté until softened, about 5 minutes.
5. Stir in the millet, corn, and lime juice and sauté until warm, 5 to 6 minutes.
6. Place the tomatoes, hollow-side up, in a medium baking dish.
7. Divide the millet mixture evenly among the tomatoes and top with the Parmesan cheese. Bake for approximately 15 minutes, or until the filling is completely heated through and the tomatoes are softened.
8. Serve topped with cilantro.

Nutrition Info:
- Info Per Serving: Calories: 464 ; Fat: 10 g ;Saturated fat: 2 g ;Sodium: 413 mg

Broccoli Stuffed Sweetato

Servings: 4
Cooking Time: 30 Min
Ingredients:

- 4 large sweet potatoes, washed
- 1 tbsp. avocado oil, divided
- 2 cups broccoli florets
- Himalayan pink salt
- Ground black pepper
- 1 (15 oz) can low-sodium black-eyed peas, drained and rinsed
- ½ cup organic tahini dressing
- 2 spring onions, finely sliced

Directions:
1. Heat the oven to 375°F gas mark 5.
2. Use a fork to pierce the sweet potatoes all over.
3. Rub the sweet potato skin with ½ tbsp. of avocado oil and place them on a baking sheet.
4. Bake for 20 to 30 minutes, or until fully cooked and easily pierced with a fork.
5. In a medium-sized mixing bowl, add the broccoli and the remaining ½ tbsp. of avocado oil, toss to coat. Season with salt and pepper to taste.
6. After 10 minutes of baking the sweet potatoes, arrange the seasoned broccoli onto the baking sheet and roast for 20 minutes, or until tender and lightly browned. Remove from the oven.
7. Cut the sweet potatoes in half lengthwise, top with the black-eyed peas and roasted broccoli.
8. Drizzle with the tahini dressing and sprinkle spring onion on top. Serve warm.

Nutrition Info:
- Info Per Serving: Calories: 368 ; Fat: 15 g ;Saturated fat: 2 g ;Sodium: 564 mg

Bean And Veggie Cassoulet

Servings: X
Cooking Time: 25 Minutes
Ingredients:

- 1 teaspoon olive oil
- ½ cup chopped sweet onion
- ½ cup chopped celery
- ½ cup shredded carrot
- 1 teaspoon minced garlic
- 1 cup low-sodium canned pinto beans, rinsed and drained
- 1 cup low-sodium canned black beans, rinsed and drained
- 1 cup low-sodium canned lentils, rinsed and drained
- 1 cup low-sodium vegetable broth
- 2 large tomatoes, chopped
- 1 cup shredded Swiss chard or collard greens
- 1 teaspoon chopped fresh oregano
- ½ teaspoon ground coriander
- Sea salt
- Freshly ground black pepper

Directions:

1. In a large saucepan, warm the oil over medium-high heat.
2. Add the onions, celery, carrots, and garlic and sauté until softened, 5 to 7 minutes.
3. Stir in the beans, lentils, and vegetable broth and bring the mixture to a boil. Reduce the heat to low and simmer 10 minutes.
4. Stir in the tomatoes, greens, oregano, and coriander and simmer until the greens are tender, about 5 minutes.
5. Season the cassoulet with salt and pepper and serve.

Nutrition Info:

- Info Per Serving: Calories: 446 ; Fat:4 g ;Saturated fat: 1 g ;Sodium: 127 mg

Pinto Bean Tortillas

Servings: 4
Cooking Time: 25 Min
Ingredients:

- 1 (15 oz) can low-sodium pinto beans, rinsed and drained
- ¼ cup canned fire-roasted tomato salsa
- ¾ cup dairy-free cheddar cheese, shredded and divided
- 1 medium red bell pepper, seeded, chopped and divided
- 2 tbsp. olive oil, divided
- 4 large, wholegrain tortillas

Directions:

1. Place the drained pinto beans and the tomato salsa together in a food processor. Process until smooth.
2. Spread ½ cup of the pinto bean mixture on each tortilla. Sprinkle each tortilla with 3 tbsp. of dairy-free cheddar cheese and ¼ cup of red bell pepper. Fold in half and repeat with the remaining tortillas.
3. Add 1 tbsp. of olive oil to a large, heavy-bottom pan over medium heat until hot. Place the first two folded tortillas in the pan. Cover and cook for 2 minutes until the tortillas are crispy on the bottom. Flip and cook for 2 minutes until crispy on the other side.
4. Repeat with the remaining folded tortillas and the remaining olive oil. Keep warm until ready to serve.

Nutrition Info:

- Info Per Serving: Calories:438 ; Fat: 21 g ;Saturated fat: 5 g ;Sodium: 561 mg

Butter Bean Rotini

Servings: 4
Cooking Time: 15 Min
Ingredients:

- 8 oz rotini pasta
- 2 tbsp. avocado oil
- 1 bunch spinach, stemmed and chopped
- 1 (15 oz) can low-sodium diced tomatoes, drained
- 1 (15 oz) can low-sodium butter beans, drained and rinsed
- 1 tsp thyme, chopped
- 1 tsp oregano, chopped
- Fine sea salt
- Ground black pepper

Directions:

1. Fill a large stockpot with water and bring to the boil.
2. Cook the pasta for 8 minutes or according to the package instructions until al dente. Remove from the heat and reserve ¼ cup of the pasta water and drain the remaining water.
3. In a large heavy-bottom pan, heat the avocado oil over medium heat until hot.
4. Add the spinach and fry for 4 to 6 minutes, or until wilted.
5. Add the tomatoes and butter beans, cook for 3 to 5 minutes, or until heated through and the tomatoes have released some of their water.
6. Season with thyme, oregano, salt and pepper.
7. Mix the cooked pasta into the pan along with the reserved water. Cook for 1 minute until heated through and starting to thicken.

Nutrition Info:

- Info Per Serving: Calories: 435 ; Fat: 9 g ;Saturated fat: 1 g ;Sodium: 208 mg

Roasted Garlic Soufflé

Servings: 4
Cooking Time: X
Ingredients:

- 1 head Roasted Garlic
- 2 tablespoons olive oil
- 1 cup finely chopped cooked turkey breast
- ¼ cup grated Parmesan cheese
- 1/8 teaspoon pepper
- 1 egg
- ¼ cup low-fat sour cream
- 6 egg whites
- ¼ teaspoon cream of tartar
- ¼ cup chopped flat-leaf parsley

Directions:

1. Preheat oven to 375ºF. Grease the bottom of a 2-quart soufflé dish with peanut oil and set aside. Squeeze the garlic from the papery skins. Discard skins, and in medium bowl, combine olive oil with the garlic. Add turkey, cheese, pepper, egg, and sour cream, and mix well.
2. In large bowl, combine egg whites with cream of tartar. Beat until stiff peaks form. Stir a spoonful of egg whites into the turkey mixture and stir well. Then fold in remaining egg whites. Fold in parsley.
3. Spoon mixture into prepared soufflé dish. Bake for 40–50 minutes or until the soufflé is puffed and golden. Serve immediately.

Nutrition Info:

- Info Per Serving: Calories:223.79 ; Fat: 14.23 g ;Saturated fat:3.92 g ;Sodium: 253.37 mg

Crisp Polenta With Tomato Sauce

Servings: 8
Cooking Time: X
Ingredients:
- 1 recipe Cheese Polenta
- 1 cup shredded part-skim mozzarella cheese
- 3 cups Spaghetti Sauce , heated

Directions:
1. Prepare polenta as directed, except when done, pour onto a greased cookie sheet; spread to a ½″-thick rectangle, about 9″ × 15″. Cover and chill until very firm, about 2 hours.
2. Preheat broiler. Cut polenta into fifteen 3″ squares. Place on broiler pan; broil for 4–6 minutes or until golden brown. Carefully turn polenta and broil for 3–5 minutes or until golden brown.
3. Remove from oven and sprinkle with mozzarella cheese. Top each with a dollop of the hot Spaghetti Sauce, and serve immediately.

Nutrition Info:
- Info Per Serving: Calories: 229.70 ; Fat:8.43 g ;Saturated fat: 4.20 g ;Sodium: 260.08 mg

Spanish Omelet

Servings: 4
Cooking Time: X
Ingredients:
- 2 tablespoons olive oil, divided
- 1 onion, minced
- 2 cloves garlic, minced
- 1 stalk celery, chopped
- ½ cup chopped red bell pepper
- 1 jalapeño pepper, minced
- ½ teaspoon dried oregano
- 2 tomatoes, chopped
- 1/8 teaspoon salt
- 1/8 teaspoon pepper
- 1 egg
- 8 egg whites
- ¼ cup skim milk
- 2 tablespoons low-fat sour cream
- ½ cup grated extra-sharp Cheddar cheese

Directions:
1. For the sauce, in a small saucepan heat 1 tablespoon olive oil over medium heat. Add onion, garlic, celery, bell pepper, and jalapeño pepper; cook and stir for 4 minutes until crisp-tender. Add oregano, tomatoes, salt, and pepper, and bring to a simmer. Reduce heat to low and simmer for 5 minutes.
2. In large bowl, combine egg, egg whites, skim milk, and sour cream and beat until combined. Heat 1 tablespoon olive oil in nonstick skillet and add egg mixture. Cook, moving spatula around pan and lifting to let uncooked mixture flow underneath, until eggs are set but still moist.
3. Sprinkle with Cheddar and top with half of the tomato sauce. Cover and cook for 2–4 minutes longer, until bottom of omelet is golden brown. Fold over, slide onto serving plate, top with remaining tomato sauce, and serve.

Nutrition Info:
- Info Per Serving: Calories: 219.98; Fat:14.03 g ;Saturated fat: 4.95 g ;Sodium: 316.92 mg

Butternut Squash, Bulgur, And Tempeh Burritos

Servings: X
Cooking Time: 15 Minutes
Ingredients:

- 1 teaspoon olive oil
- 1 cup chopped butternut squash
- ½ cup chopped onion
- ½ cup cooked bulgur
- ½ cup crumbled tempeh
- ½ teaspoon chili powder
- ¼ teaspoon ground cumin
- 4 (6-inch) whole-grain tortillas
- ½ cup low-sodium tomato or mango salsa
- 1 scallion, white and green parts, sliced
- ½ cup shredded lettuce
- ¼ cup fat-free sour cream

Directions:
1. In a medium skillet, warm the olive oil over medium-high heat.
2. Add the squash and onions and sauté until tender, 8 to 10 minutes.
3. Add the bulgur, tempeh, chili powder, and cumin and sauté until the bulgur is heated through, about 7 minutes.
4. Wrap the tortillas in a clean kitchen towel and heat in the microwave for 15 to 30 seconds.
5. Lay the tortillas out and evenly divide the squash mixture between them. Top each with the salsa, scallion, lettuce, and sour cream.
6. Wrap the tortillas around the filling and serve.

Nutrition Info:
- Info Per Serving: Calories: 423 ; Fat: 13 g ;Saturated fat: 2 g ;Sodium: 712 mg

Risotto With Artichokes

Servings: 6
Cooking Time: X
Ingredients:

- 2 cups water
- 2½ cups low-sodium vegetable broth
- 2 tablespoons olive oil
- 4 shallots, minced
- 3 cloves garlic, minced
- 1 (10-ounce) box frozen artichoke hearts, thawed
- 1½ cups Arborio rice
- 1/8 teaspoon pepper
- ¼ cup grated Parmesan cheese
- 1 tablespoon butter
- ½ cup chopped fresh basil leaves

Directions:
1. In medium saucepan, combine water and broth; heat over low heat until warm; keep on heat.
2. In large saucepan, heat olive oil over medium heat. Add shallots and garlic; cook and stir until crisp-tender, about 4 minutes. Add artichokes; cook and stir for 3 minutes.
3. Add rice; cook and stir for 2 minutes. Add the broth mixture, a cup at a time, stirring until the liquid is absorbed, about 20–25 minutes. Stir in pepper, Parmesan, butter, and basil; cover and let stand for 5 minutes off the heat. Serve immediately.

Nutrition Info:
- Info Per Serving: Calories:317.17 ; Fat: 8.90 g ;Saturated fat:2.86g ;Sodium: 223.71 mg

Pumpkin And Chickpea Patties

Servings: X
Cooking Time: 20 Minutes
Ingredients:

- 2 teaspoons olive oil, divided
- 2 cups grated fresh pumpkin
- ½ cup grated carrot
- ½ teaspoon minced garlic
- 2 cups low-sodium chickpeas, rinsed and drained
- ½ cup ground almonds
- 2 large egg whites
- 1 scallion, white and green parts, chopped
- ½ teaspoon chopped fresh thyme
- Sea salt
- Freshly ground black pepper

Directions:

1. Preheat the oven to 400°F.
2. Line a baking sheet with parchment paper and set aside.
3. In a large skillet, heat ½ teaspoon olive oil over medium-high heat. Add the pumpkin, carrots, and garlic and sauté until softened, about 4 minutes. Remove from the heat and transfer to a food processor. Wipe the skillet clean with paper towels.
4. Add the chickpeas, almonds, egg whites, scallions, and thyme to the food processor. Pulse until the mixture holds together when pressed.
5. Season with salt and pepper and divide the pumpkin mixture into 8 equal patties, flattening them to about ½-inch thick.
6. Heat the remaining 1½ teaspoons olive oil in the skillet. Cook the patties until lightly browned, about 4 minutes on each side.
7. Place the skillet in the oven and bake for an additional 5 minutes, until the patties are completely heated through.
8. Serve.

Nutrition Info:

- Info Per Serving: Calories: 560 ; Fat: 25 g ;Saturated fat: 3 g ;Sodium: 62 mg

Chopped Vegetable Tabbouleh

Servings: X
Cooking Time: X
Ingredients:

- 2 cups cooked quinoa
- 2 cup finely chopped cauliflower
- ½ cup shelled edamame
- 2 tomatoes, chopped
- ½ English cucumber, chopped
- 1 scallion, white and green parts, thinly sliced
- ¼ cup chopped fresh parsley
- 2 tablespoons chopped fresh mint
- Juice and zest of 1 lemon
- Sea salt
- Freshly ground black pepper

Directions:

1. In a medium bowl, toss together the quinoa, cauliflower, edamame, tomatoes, cucumber, scallions, parsley, mint, lemon juice, and lemon zest.
2. Season with salt and pepper.
3. Serve.

Nutrition Info:

- Info Per Serving: Calories: 430 ; Fat:8 g ;Saturated fat: 1 g ;Sodium: 58 mg

Potato Soufflé

Servings: 4
Cooking Time: X
Ingredients:

- 2 Yukon Gold potatoes
- 1 tablespoon olive oil
- 1/8 teaspoon nutmeg
- ¼ teaspoon onion salt
- 1/8 teaspoon cayenne pepper
- 1/3 cup fat-free half-and-half
- ¼ cup grated Parmesan cheese
- 4 egg whites
- ¼ teaspoon cream of tartar
- 1 cup chopped grape tomatoes
- ¼ cup chopped fresh basil

Directions:
1. Preheat oven to 450ºF. Peel and thinly slice potatoes, adding to a pot of cold water as you work. Bring potatoes to a boil over high heat, reduce heat, and simmer until tender, about 12–15 minutes.
2. Drain potatoes and return to hot pot; shake for 1 minute. Add olive oil, nutmeg, salt, and pepper and mash until smooth. Beat in the half-and-half and Parmesan.
3. In large bowl, combine egg whites with cream of tartar and beat until stiff peaks form. Stir a dollop of the egg whites into the potato mixture and stir. Then fold in remaining egg whites.
4. Spray the bottom of a 2-quart casserole with nonstick cooking spray. Spoon potato mixture into casserole. Bake for 20 minutes, then reduce heat to 375ºF and bake for another 12–17 minutes or until soufflé is golden brown and puffed.
5. While soufflé is baking, combine tomatoes and basil in small bowl and mix gently. Serve immediately with tomato mixture for topping the soufflé.

Nutrition Info:
- Info Per Serving: Calories: 224.39; Fat:9.11 g ;Saturated fat:2.24 g ;Sodium: 260.97 mg

Spaghetti Squash Skillet

Servings: X
Cooking Time: 35 Minutes
Ingredients:

- 1 (2-pound) spaghetti squash
- 1 tablespoon olive oil, divided
- Sea salt
- Freshly ground black pepper
- ½ cup chopped sweet onion
- 1 teaspoon minced garlic
- 1 orange bell pepper, diced
- 16 asparagus spears, woody ends trimmed, cut into 2-inch pieces
- ½ cup sliced sun-dried tomatoes
- 2 cups shredded kale
- 1 tablespoon chopped fresh basil

Directions:
1. Preheat the oven to 400°F.
2. Line a baking sheet with parchment paper and set aside.
3. Slice the squash in half lengthwise and scoop out the seeds. Place the squash, cut-side up, on the baking sheet. Brush the cut edges and hollows with 1 teaspoon olive oil and season lightly with salt and pepper.
4. Roast the squash until a knife can be inserted easily into the thickest section, 30 to 35 minutes.
5. Remove from the oven and let the squash cool for 10 minutes, then use a fork to shred the flesh into a medium bowl. Set aside.
6. While the squash is cooling, warm the remaining 2 teaspoons olive oil in a medium skillet over medium heat. Add the onions and garlic and sauté until softened, about 3 minutes.
7. Stir in the bell pepper, asparagus, sun-dried tomatoes, and kale and sauté until the vegetables and greens are tender, about 5 minutes.
8. Add the shredded spaghetti squash and basil and toss to combine.
9. Serve.

Nutrition Info:
- Info Per Serving: Calories: 340 ; Fat:10 g ;Saturated fat: 2 g ;Sodium: 287 mg

Kidney Bean Stew

Servings: 4
Cooking Time: 25 Min
Ingredients:
- 2 tsp avocado oil
- 1 leek, thinly sliced
- ½ brown onion, finely chopped
- 1 tsp garlic, minced
- 3 cups low-sodium vegetable stock
- 1 cup Roma tomatoes, chopped
- 2 medium carrots, peeled and thinly sliced
- 1 cup cauliflower florets
- 1 cup broccoli florets
- 1 green bell pepper, seeds removed and diced
- 1 cup low-sodium canned kidney beans, rinsed and drained
- Pinch red pepper flakes
- Himalayan pink salt
- Ground black pepper
- 2 tbsp. low-fat Parmesan cheese, grated for garnish
- 1 tbsp. parsley, chopped for garnish

Directions:
1. In a large-sized stockpot, warm the avocado oil over medium-high heat.
2. Add the sliced leek, chopped onions, and minced garlic and fry for 4 minutes until softened.
3. Add the vegetable stock, tomatoes, carrots, cauliflower, broccoli, green bell peppers, kidney beans, and red pepper flakes, mix to combine.
4. Bring the stew to a boil, then reduce the heat to low and simmer for 18 to 20 minutes until the vegetables are tender.
5. Season with salt and pepper to taste.
6. Top with Parmesan cheese and parsley.

Nutrition Info:
- Info Per Serving: Calories:270 ; Fat: 8g ;Saturated fat: 3g ;Sodium: 237 mg

Quinoa Pepper Pilaf

Servings: 6
Cooking Time: X
Ingredients:
- 2 tablespoons olive oil
- 2 Italian frying peppers, chopped
- 1 green bell pepper, chopped
- 1 red bell pepper, chopped
- 1 onion, chopped
- 4 garlic cloves, minced
- ¼ cup chopped sun-dried tomatoes
- 1/8 teaspoon salt
- 1/8 teaspoon white pepper
- 1¼ cups quinoa
- 2½ cups low-sodium vegetable broth

Directions:
1. In large saucepan, heat olive oil over medium heat. Add frying peppers, green bell pepper, red bell pepper, onion, and garlic; cook and stir until crisp-tender, about 4 minutes. Add sun-dried tomatoes, salt, pepper, and quinoa; cook and stir for 2 minutes.
2. Pour in 1½ cups broth and bring to a simmer. Reduce heat to medium low and cook, stirring frequently, until the broth is absorbed, about 7 minutes. Add remaining broth and cook, stirring frequently, until quinoa is tender. Cover and remove from heat; let stand for 5 minutes. Fluff with a fork and serve.

Nutrition Info:
- Info Per Serving: Calories:241.29; Fat: 8.16 g ;Saturated fat: 1.14 g ;Sodium: 199.17 mg

Soups, Salads, And Sides

Caramelized Spiced Carrots

Servings: 6
Cooking Time: X
Ingredients:

- 1¼ pounds baby carrots
- ¼ cup orange juice
- 1/8 teaspoon salt
- 1/8 teaspoon white pepper
- 1 teaspoon grated orange zest
- 1 tablespoon sugar
- 1 tablespoon grated ginger root
- 1 tablespoon butter or plant sterol margarine

Directions:

1. In large saucepan, combine carrots, orange juice, salt, and pepper. Bring to a boil over high heat, then reduce heat to low, cover, and cook for 3–4 minutes or until carrots are crisp-tender.
2. Add orange zest, sugar, ginger root, and butter and bring to a boil over high heat. Cook until most of the orange juice evaporates and the carrots start to brown, stirring frequently, about 4–5 minutes. Serve immediately.

Nutrition Info:

- Info Per Serving: Calories: 62.66 ; Fat: 2.07 g ;Saturated fat: 1.24 g ;Sodium: 135.88 mg

Roasted Garlic

Servings: 6
Cooking Time: X
Ingredients:

- 1 head garlic
- 2 teaspoons olive oil Pinch salt
- 1 teaspoon lemon juice

Directions:

1. Preheat oven to 400ºF. Peel off some of the outer skins from the garlic head, leaving the head whole. Cut off the top ½" of the garlic head; discard top.
2. Place on a square of heavy-duty aluminum foil, cut side up. Drizzle with the olive oil, making sure the oil runs into the cloves. Sprinkle with salt and lemon juice.
3. Wrap garlic in the foil, covering completely. Place on a baking sheet and roast for 40–50 minutes or until garlic is very soft and golden brown. Let cool for 15 minutes, then serve or use in recipes.

Nutrition Info:

- Info Per Serving: Calories: 32.10; Fat:1.56 g ;Saturated fat:0.22 g ;Sodium:28.00 mg

Asparagus With Almond Topping

Servings: X
Cooking Time: 5 Minutes
Ingredients:

- ½ teaspoon avocado oil
- ½ cup finely chopped almonds
- Juice and zest of ½ lime
- Sea salt
- Freshly ground black pepper
- ½ pound asparagus, woody ends trimmed

Directions:

1. In a small skillet, warm the olive oil over medium heat.
2. Add the almonds and sauté until they are fragrant and golden brown, about 4 minutes.
3. Remove from the heat and stir in the lime zest and juice.
4. Season the almond mixture with salt and pepper and set aside.
5. Fill a medium saucepan with water and bring to a boil over high heat.
6. Blanch the asparagus until tender-crisp, about 2 minutes.
7. Drain the asparagus and arrange it on a serving plate.
8. Sprinkle the almond topping over the vegetables and serve.

Nutrition Info:

- Info Per Serving: Calories: 192 ; Fat: 15 g ;Saturated fat: 1 g ;Sodium: 10 mg

Gazpacho

Servings: 4
Cooking Time: 20 Minutes
Ingredients:

- 4 large beefsteak tomatoes, chopped
- 1 cup yellow or red cherry tomatoes, chopped
- 1 cup grape tomatoes, chopped
- 1 cucumber, peeled, seeded, and chopped
- 3 scallions, sliced
- 1 clove garlic, minced
- 1 cup low-sodium tomato juice
- 1 tablespoon fresh lemon juice
- 1 tablespoon olive oil
- Pinch salt
- ⅛ teaspoon white pepper
- Dash Tabasco sauce
- 2 tablespoons chopped fresh dill

Directions:

1. In a large bowl, combine the beefsteak tomatoes, cherry tomatoes, grape tomatoes, cucumber, scallions, garlic, tomato juice, lemon juice, olive oil, salt, white pepper, Tabasco, and fresh dill.
2. Use an immersion blender to blend about half of the soup. You can also mash some of the ingredients with a potato masher. Or put about ⅓ of the soup mixture into a blender or food processor. Blend or process until smooth, then return the blended mixture to the rest of the soup.
3. Serve immediately, or cover and chill for a few hours.

Nutrition Info:

- Info Per Serving: Calories: 115 ; Fat: 4 g ;Saturated fat: 1 g ;Sodium: 225 mg

Apple Coleslaw

Servings: 6
Cooking Time: X
Ingredients:

- 1 cup plain yogurt
- ¼ cup low-fat mayonnaise
- ¼ cup buttermilk
- 2 tablespoons mustard
- 2 tablespoons lemon juice
- 1 tablespoon chopped fresh tarragon leaves
- 2 Granny Smith apples, chopped
- 3 cups shredded red cabbage
- 3 cups shredded green cabbage
- ½ cup walnut pieces, toasted

Directions:

1. In large bowl, combine yogurt, mayonnaise, buttermilk, mustard, lemon juice, and tarragon leaves; mix well to blend. Add chopped apples, red cabbage, and green cabbage and mix well.
2. Cover and chill in refrigerator for 2–4 hours before serving. Sprinkle with walnuts before serving.

Nutrition Info:

- Info Per Serving: Calories: 184.33; Fat:10.59 g ;Saturated fat:1.36 g;Sodium: 188.36 mg

Cucumber-mango Salad

Servings: 4
Cooking Time: X
Ingredients:

- ½ cup plain yogurt
- ¼ cup buttermilk
- 2 tablespoons lemon juice
- 1 tablespoon honey
- 2 tablespoons chopped fresh dill
- ½ cup finely chopped red onion
- 2 cucumbers
- 2 ripe mangoes

Directions:
1. In large bowl, combine yogurt, buttermilk, lemon juice, honey, dill, and onion and mix well with wire whisk.
2. Peel cucumbers and cut in half lengthwise; using a spoon, scoop out the seeds. Cut into ¼" slices and add to yogurt mixture.
3. Peel mangoes and, standing them on end, slice down around the pit to remove the flesh. Cut into cubes and add to yogurt mixture; toss gently and serve, or chill for 2–3 hours before serving.

Nutrition Info:
- Info Per Serving: Calories:119.80; Fat: 1.13 g ;Saturated fat:0.48 g ;Sodium:43.06 mg

Sesame Spinach

Servings: 3
Cooking Time: 2 Minutes
Ingredients:

- ½ pound spinach leaves
- 1 teaspoon minced garlic
- ½ tablespoon sesame oil
- Sea salt
- Freshly ground black pepper
- Sesame seeds

Directions:
1. Place a medium stockpot filled three-quarters full of water over high heat and bring to a boil.
2. Add the spinach and let boil for 1 to 2 minutes until softened.
3. Use a strainer to separate the spinach from the water and let cool. Then use your hands to squeeze out as much liquid from the spinach as possible.
4. Cut the spinach into bite-size pieces and transfer it to a medium bowl.
5. Add the garlic and sesame oil and season with salt and pepper.
6. Sprinkle with sesame seeds and serve immediately.

Nutrition Info:
- Info Per Serving: Calories: 56; Fat: 4 g ;Saturated fat: 1 g ;Sodium: 113 mg

Roasted-garlic Corn

Servings: 6
Cooking Time: X
Ingredients:

- 3 cups frozen corn, thawed
- 2 tablespoons olive oil
- 2 shallots, minced
- 1 head Roasted Garlic
- 1/8 teaspoon salt
- 1/8 teaspoon white pepper

Directions:
1. Preheat oven to 425ºF. Place corn on paper towels and pat to dry. Place a Silpat liner on a 15″ × 10″ jelly-roll pan. Combine corn, olive oil, and shallots on pan and toss to coat. Spread in even layer.
2. Roast corn for 14–22 minutes, stirring once during cooking time, until kernels begin to turn light golden brown in spots.
3. Remove cloves from Roasted Garlic and add to corn along with salt and white pepper. Stir to mix, then serve.

Nutrition Info:
- Info Per Serving: Calories:147.64 ; Fat: 6.70 g ;Saturated fat: 0.94 g;Sodium: 79.60 mg

Fruity Rice Salad

Servings: 6
Cooking Time: X
Ingredients:
- 2 tablespoons chopped fresh mint
- 1 cup low-fat strawberry yogurt
- 1 tablespoon lemon juice
- 2 tablespoons skim milk
- 1 cup cooked brown rice, chilled
- 1 cup cooked white rice, chilled
- 1 (15-ounce) can crushed pineapple, drained
- 1 banana, sliced
- 2 cups chopped strawberries
- 1 cup blueberries

Directions:
1. In large bowl, combine mint, yogurt, lemon juice, and skim milk and mix well. Add both types of rice and mix until combined. Then fold in remaining fruit. Cover and chill for 2–4 hours before serving.

Nutrition Info:
- Info Per Serving: Calories:186.12; Fat:0.96 g ;Saturated fat:0.26 g;Sodium: 17.22 mg

Cabbage-tomato-bean Chowder

Servings: 4
Cooking Time: X
Ingredients:
- 1 tablespoon olive oil
- 1 onion, chopped
- 4 cloves garlic, minced
- 3 cups shredded green cabbage
- 1 (14-ounce) can no-salt diced tomatoes, undrained
- 1 (6-ounce) can no-salt tomato paste
- 2 cups Low-Sodium Chicken Broth
- 1 teaspoon sugar
- 1/8 teaspoon white pepper
- 2 cups Beans for Soup
- 1/3 cup fat-free half-and-half

Directions:
1. In large saucepan, heat olive oil over medium heat. Add onion and garlic; cook and stir until crisp-tender, about 4 minutes. Add cabbage; cook and stir for 3 minutes longer.
2. Add tomatoes, tomato paste, chicken broth, sugar, and pepper. Cook and stir until tomato paste dissolves in soup. Then stir in beans and bring to a simmer. Simmer for 10 minutes, then add half-and-half. Heat until the soup steams, and serve.

Nutrition Info:
- Info Per Serving: Calories: 272.75 ; Fat: 4.96 g ;Saturated fat:0.95 g ;Sodium: 148.66 mg

Hearty Bean And Quinoa Stew

Servings: 4
Cooking Time: 20 Minutes
Ingredients:
- ½ tablespoon olive oil
- 1½ tablespoons minced garlic
- 1 cup diced carrots
- Pinch sea salt
- Pinch freshly ground black pepper
- 3 cups water
- ½ cup dry quinoa
- 1 (27-ounce) can no-salt-added diced tomatoes
- 1 (18-ounce) can no-salt-added red kidney beans, drained and rinsed

Directions:
1. In a medium pot, heat the olive oil over high heat. Add the garlic, carrots, salt, and pepper and sauté for 3 minutes, until fragrant.
2. To the same pot, add the water, quinoa, tomatoes with their juices, and beans. Increase the heat to high and bring to a boil.
3. Once the mixture comes to a boil, lower the heat to medium and simmer until the quinoa is soft, about 15 minutes. Serve immediately.

Nutrition Info:
- Info Per Serving: Calories: 248 ; Fat: 3g ;Saturated fat: 1g ;Sodium: 188 mg

Butternut Squash And Lentil Soup

Servings: 4
Cooking Time: 20 Minutes
Ingredients:
- 1 tablespoon olive oil
- 1 onion, chopped
- 1 tablespoon peeled grated fresh ginger root
- 1 (12-ounce) package peeled and diced butternut squash
- 1 cup red lentils, rinsed and sorted
- 5 cups low-sodium vegetable broth
- 1 cup unsweetened apple juice
- Pinch salt
- ⅛ teaspoon black pepper
- ¼ teaspoon curry powder
- 1 sprig fresh thyme
- 3 tablespoons crumbled blue cheese

Directions:
1. In a large saucepan, heat the olive oil over medium heat. Add the onion, and cook and stir for 3 minutes. Add the ginger, squash, and lentils, and cook and stir for 1 minute.
2. Turn up the heat to medium-high, and add the broth, apple juice, salt, pepper, curry powder, and thyme. Bring the mixture to a boil.
3. Reduce the heat to low and partially cover the pan. Simmer for 15 to 18 minutes or until the squash and lentils are tender. Remove the thyme sprig; the leaves will have fallen off.
4. Purée the soup, either in a food processor, with an immersion blender, or with a potato masher. Heat again, then ladle into bowls, sprinkle with the blue cheese, and serve warm.

Nutrition Info:
- Info Per Serving: Calories: 317 ; Fat: 7g ;Saturated fat: 2g ;Sodium:280 mg

Chinese Skewered Chicken

Servings: 6–8
Cooking Time: X
Ingredients:
- 2 tablespoons olive oil
- 2 tablespoons dry sherry or apple juice
- 1 tablespoon low-sodium soy sauce
- 1 teaspoon sesame oil
- 1 teaspoon five-spice powder
- 1 tablespoon honey
- 1 tablespoon minced ginger root
- 2 cloves garlic, minced
- ½ teaspoon cayenne pepper
- 1 pound chicken tenders
- 2 green bell peppers, sliced

Directions:
1. In medium bowl, combine olive oil, sherry, soy sauce, sesame oil, five-spice powder, honey, ginger root, garlic, and cayenne pepper and mix well.
2. Cut tenders crosswise into 3 pieces each. Add to olive oil mixture, stir well, cover, and refrigerate for at least 4 hours.
3. When ready to serve, prepare and preheat grill. Thread chicken pieces and bell pepper strips on metal skewers. Grill 6″ from medium coals, turning once, until chicken is thoroughly cooked. Brush food once with marinade during cooking time, then discard marinade. Serve immediately.

Nutrition Info:
- Info Per Serving: Calories:122.72; Fat: 4.20 g ;Saturated fat: 0.87 g ;Sodium: 115.36 mg

Summer Pineapple Fruit Salad

Servings: 8
Cooking Time: X
Ingredients:
- 1 cup lemon yogurt
- ¼ cup nonfat whipped salad dressing
- 1 teaspoon lemon zest
- 2 tablespoons honey
- 1 teaspoon chopped fresh thyme
- 1 fresh pineapple
- 1 cantaloupe
- 1 honeydew melon
- 2 cups sliced strawberries
- 1 pint blueberries
- 1 cup raspberries

Directions:
1. In large bowl, combine yogurt, salad dressing, lemon zest, and honey, and mix well. Stir in thyme and set aside.
2. Twist top off pineapple and discard. Slice pineapple in half, then cut off rind. Cut into quarters, then cut out center core. Slice pineapple and add to yogurt mixture.
3. Cut cantaloupe and melon in half, scoop out seeds and discard, and peel. Cut into cubes and add to yogurt mixture along with strawberries and blueberries. Toss gently and top with raspberries. Serve immediately, or cover and refrigerate up to 4 hours.

Nutrition Info:
- Info Per Serving: Calories:201.31; Fat:3.63 g ;Saturated fat:0.73 g;Sodium: 94.22 mg

Minestrone Florentine Soup

Servings: X
Cooking Time: 25 Minutes
Ingredients:

- 1 teaspoon olive oil
- 1 celery stalk, diced
- 1 carrot, thinly sliced
- ¼ sweet onion, peeled and chopped
- 1 teaspoon minced garlic
- 3 cups low-sodium vegetable broth
- 1 cup low-sodium canned diced tomatoes, with their juices
- 1 cup low-sodium canned cannellini beans, rinsed and drained
- 1 cup fresh baby spinach
- 1 teaspoon chopped fresh basil
- Pinch red pepper flakes
- Sea salt
- Freshly ground black pepper

Directions:

1. In a medium saucepan, warm the olive oil over medium-high heat.
2. Add the celery, carrots, onions, and garlic and sauté until softened, about 5 minutes.
3. Stir in the vegetable broth, tomatoes, and beans and bring the soup to a boil.
4. Reduce the heat to low and simmer until the vegetables are tender, about 15 minutes.
5. Remove the soup from the heat and stir in the spinach, basil, and red pepper flakes. Let stand for 5 minutes to allow the spinach to wilt. Season with salt and pepper and serve.

Nutrition Info:

- Info Per Serving: Calories: 190 ; Fat: 3 g ;Saturated fat: 0 g ;Sodium: 151 mg

Garbanzo Bean Pops

Servings: 4
Cooking Time: 30 Min
Ingredients:

- Aluminum foil
- 1 (15 oz) can garbanzo beans, drained and rinsed
- 1 tsp avocado oil
- ¼ tsp ground cumin
- ¼ tsp paprika
- Pinch red pepper flakes
- Himalayan pink Salt
- Ground black pepper

Directions:

1. Heat the oven to 400°F gas mark 6. Line a baking sheet with aluminum foil.
2. Use a clean tea towel to dry the garbanzo beans well. Discard any loose skin.
3. Place the garbanzo beans on the baking sheet and drizzle with avocado oil, toss to coat.
4. Place the baking sheet in the oven and roast for 25 to 30 minutes, until the garbanzo beans are crispy and browned. Remove from the oven.
5. Add the cumin, paprika, red pepper flakes, salt and pepper to taste, toss to combine.

Nutrition Info:

- Info Per Serving: Calories: 89 ; Fat:3 g ;Saturated fat: 0g ;Sodium: 160 mg

Nuts On The Go

Servings: 3
Cooking Time: X
Ingredients:

- 1 cup unsalted mixed nuts
- ⅔ cup dried cranberries
- ½ cup coconut flakes, toasted
- ½ cup banana chips
- ¼ cup 60% dark chocolate chips (optional)

Directions:

1. Place the nuts, cranberries, coconut flakes, banana chips, and chocolate chips (if using) into an airtight container, mix to combine.
2. Keep for up to 1 week on the counter or for 3 months in the freezer.

Nutrition Info:

- Info Per Serving: Calories: 174 ; Fat:12 g ;Saturated fat: 2g ;Sodium: 18 mg

Carrot Peach Soup

Servings: 4
Cooking Time: 15 Minutes
Ingredients:

- 2 large carrots, peeled and chopped
- 2 peaches, peeled and chopped (see Ingredient Tip)
- 2 cups water
- ½ cup orange juice
- 2 tablespoons honey
- 1 sprig fresh thyme leaves
- Pinch salt
- ⅓ cup plain low-fat Greek yogurt

Directions:

1. In a large saucepan, combine the carrots, peaches, water, orange juice, honey, thyme, and salt, and bring to a simmer over medium heat.
2. Simmer the mixture for 7 to 9 minutes or until the carrots are tender.
3. Add the yogurt to the soup and remove the thyme sprig. Purée the soup, either with an immersion blender directly in the pot, or pour the soup in two batches into a blender or food processor, and holding a towel over the lid, carefully blend until smooth. Serve immediately or cover and chill for 2 hours.

Nutrition Info:

- Info Per Serving: Calories:102 ; Fat: 0 g ;Saturated fat: 0 g ;Sodium: 77 mg

Veggie-stuffed Tomatoes

Servings: 4
Cooking Time: X
Ingredients:

- 1 tablespoon olive oil
- 1 onion, chopped
- 3 cloves garlic, minced
- 1 green bell pepper, chopped
- 4 stalks celery, chopped
- 1 tablespoon chopped fresh chives
- 2 teaspoons fresh oregano leaves
- 1/8 teaspoon salt
- 1/8 teaspoon pepper
- ½ cup plain yogurt
- 1 tablespoon lime juice
- 2 tablespoons grated Parmesan cheese
- 4 large tomatoes

Directions:

1. In medium saucepan, heat olive oil over medium heat. Add onion, garlic, and green bell pepper; cook and stir until crisp-tender, about 4 minutes. Remove from heat and stir in celery, chives, oregano, salt, and pepper. Remove to medium bowl and chill until cold, about 1 hour.
2. Stir yogurt, lime juice, and Parmesan into cooled vegetable mixture. Cut tops off tomatoes and gently scoop out tomato flesh and seeds, leaving a ½" shell. Stuff with the vegetable mixture. Cover and chill for 2–3 hours before serving.

Nutrition Info:

- Info Per Serving: Calories:122.14; Fat:5.75 g ;Saturated fat: 1.74 g;Sodium: 194.39 mg

Speedy Chicken Alphabet Soup

Servings: X
Cooking Time: 20 Minutes
Ingredients:
- 1 teaspoon olive oil
- 2 celery stalks, thinly sliced
- ½ small sweet onion, peeled and chopped
- ½ teaspoon minced garlic
- 4 cups low-sodium chicken broth
- 2 carrots, diced
- 1 cup diced cooked chicken breast
- ½ cup dry alphabet pasta
- 1 teaspoon chopped fresh thyme
- ½ cup shredded Swiss chard
- Freshly ground black pepper

Directions:
1. In a medium saucepan, warm the olive oil over medium-high heat.
2. Add the celery, onions, and garlic and sauté until softened, about 4 minutes.
3. Stir in the broth, carrots, chicken, pasta, and thyme. Bring to a boil, then reduce the heat to low and simmer the soup until the noodles are cooked through and the vegetables are tender, about 15 minutes.
4. Stir in the chard and season the soup with pepper.
5. Serve.

Nutrition Info:
- Info Per Serving: Calories: 233 ; Fat: 5 g ;Saturated fat: 1 g ;Sodium: 290 mg

Garbanzo Bean Salad

Servings: 6
Cooking Time: 15 Min
Ingredients:
- 3 tbsp. avocado olive oil, divided
- 2 tbsp. balsamic vinegar
- ½ tsp fine sea salt, divided
- ¼ tsp ground black pepper
- 1 cup Israeli couscous
- 1 cup water
- 2 cups grape tomatoes, halved
- ¼ cup black olives, pitted and sliced
- 1 (15 oz) can garbanzo beans, drained and rinsed
- ¼ cup parsley, chopped

Directions:
1. In a small Pyrex jug, add 2 tbsp. of avocado oil, balsamic vinegar, ¼ tsp salt, and black pepper, whisk to combine. Set aside.
2. Heat the remaining 1 tbsp. avocado oil in a large heavy-bottom pan over medium-high heat.
3. Add the Israeli couscous and cook for 2 minutes, stirring frequently, until lightly browned. Add the water and allow to boil.
4. Mix in the remaining ¼ tsp salt. Reduce the heat to low and simmer. Cook for 10 minutes, or until tender. Remove from the heat and drain. Set aside to cool.
5. In a large-sized serving bowl, add the tomato halves, garbanzo beans, and the vinaigrette, mix to combine.
6. Add the cooked couscous and mix to incorporate. Leave it to cool to room temperature.
7. Mix in the chopped parsley and serve.

Nutrition Info:
- Info Per Serving: Calories: 231 ; Fat:8g ;Saturated fat: 1g ;Sodium: 282 mg

Red Lentil Soup

Servings: 4
Cooking Time: X
Ingredients:

- 2 tablespoons olive oil
- 4 cloves garlic, minced
- 1 cup chopped onion
- 2 tablespoons minced ginger root
- 2 parsnips, peeled and chopped
- 3 carrots, peeled and chopped
- 2 cups vegetable broth
- 2 cups water
- 2 sprigs fresh thyme
- 1 cup red lentils

Directions:

1. In large soup pot, heat olive oil over medium heat. Add garlic and onion; cook and stir until crisp-tender, about 4 minutes. Add ginger root, parsnips, and carrots and cook for 2 minutes. Then stir in vegetable broth, water, and thyme sprigs and bring to a boil. Reduce heat, cover, and simmer for 10 minutes.

2. Meanwhile, pick over lentils and wash thoroughly. Add lentils to pot and bring back to a simmer. Simmer for 15–25 minutes or until lentils and vegetables are tender. Remove the thyme stems and discard. You can puree this soup if you'd like, but you can also serve just as it is.

Nutrition Info:

- Info Per Serving: Calories:271.98 ; Fat: 8.05g ;Saturated fat:1.24 g ;Sodium: 41.12 mg

Sauces, Dressings, And Staples

Tzatziki

Servings: 4
Cooking Time: X
Ingredients:

- 1¼ cups plain low-fat Greek yogurt
- 1 cucumber, peeled, seeded, and diced
- 2 tablespoons fresh lime juice
- ½ teaspoon grated fresh lime zest
- 2 cloves garlic, minced
- Pinch salt
- ⅛ teaspoon white pepper
- 1 tablespoon minced fresh dill
- 1 tablespoon minced fresh mint
- 2 teaspoons olive oil

Directions:
1. In a medium bowl, combine the yogurt, cucumber, lime juice, lime zest, garlic, salt, white pepper, dill, and mint.
2. Transfer the mixture to a serving bowl. Drizzle with the olive oil.
3. Serve immediately or store in an airtight glass container and refrigerate for up to 2 days

Nutrition Info:
- Info Per Serving: Calories: 100 ; Fat: 4 g ;Saturated fat: 1 g ;Sodium: 56 mg

Fresh Lime Salsa

Servings: 5
Cooking Time: X
Ingredients:

- 3 tomatoes, coarsely chopped
- ¼ cup chopped white onion
- ¼ cup chopped fresh cilantro
- 1 tablespoon minced garlic
- 1 tablespoon freshly squeezed lime juice
- Sea salt

Directions:
1. In a blender, place the tomatoes, onion, cilantro, garlic, and lime juice and blend until smooth. Season with salt and use immediately.

Nutrition Info:
- Info Per Serving: Calories: 20; Fat: 0 g ;Saturated fat: 0 g ;Sodium: 36 mg

Double Tomato Sauce

Servings: 3
Cooking Time: 35 Minutes
Ingredients:

- 1 teaspoon olive oil
- ½ sweet onion, chopped
- 2 teaspoons minced garlic
- 1 (28-ounce) can low-sodium diced tomatoes with their juices
- ½ cup chopped sun-dried tomatoes
- Pinch red pepper flakes
- 2 tablespoons chopped fresh basil
- 2 tablespoons chopped fresh parsley
- Sea salt
- Freshly ground black pepper
- Whole-grain pasta or zucchini noodles, for serving (optional)

Directions:
1. In a large saucepan, warm the olive oil over medium-high heat.
2. Add the onions and garlic and sauté until softened, about 3 minutes.
3. Stir in the tomatoes, sun-dried tomatoes, and red pepper flakes and bring the sauce to a simmer.
4. Reduce the heat and simmer for 20 to 25 minutes.
5. Stir in the basil and parsley and simmer for 5 more minutes.
6. Season with salt and pepper.
7. Serve over whole-grain pasta or zucchini noodles.

Nutrition Info:
- Info Per Serving: Calories:94 ; Fat: 1 g ;Saturated fat: 0 g ;Sodium: 243mg

Lemon-cilantro Vinaigrette

Servings: ⅓
Cooking Time: X
Ingredients:

- 2 tablespoons freshly squeezed lemon juice
- 2 tablespoons chopped fresh cilantro
- 2 tablespoons chopped jalapeño pepper
- 1 teaspoon honey
- ½ teaspoon minced garlic
- Pinch sea salt
- Pinch freshly ground black pepper
- Pinch cayenne pepper
- ¼ cup olive oil

Directions:
1. In a blender, add the lemon juice, cilantro, jalapeños, honey, garlic, salt, pepper, and cayenne and pulse until very smooth.
2. Turn the blender on and pour in the olive oil in a thin stream.

Nutrition Info:

- Info Per Serving: Calories: 117 ; Fat: 13 g ;Saturated fat: 2 g ;Sodium: 60 mg

Mustard Berry Vinaigrette

Servings: 8
Cooking Time: 10 Minutes
Ingredients:

- 3 tablespoons low-sodium yellow mustard
- ½ cup fresh raspberries
- ½ cup sliced fresh strawberries
- 2 tablespoons raspberry vinegar
- 2 teaspoons agave nectar
- Pinch salt

Directions:
1. In a blender or food processor, combine the mustard, raspberries, strawberries, raspberry vinegar, agave nectar, and salt, and blend or process until smooth. You can also combine the ingredients in a bowl and mash them with the back of a fork.
2. Store the vinaigrette in an airtight glass container in the refrigerator for up to 3 days.

Nutrition Info:

- Info Per Serving: Calories: 27 ; Fat: 1 g ;Saturated fat: 0 g ;Sodium: 65 mg

Green Sauce

Servings: 4
Cooking Time: 15 Minutes
Ingredients:

- 1 cup watercress
- ½ cup frozen baby peas, thawed
- ¼ cup chopped fresh cilantro leaves
- 2 scallions, chopped
- 3 tablespoons silken tofu
- 2 tablespoons fresh lime juice
- 1 tablespoon green olive slices
- 1 teaspoon grated fresh lime zest
- Pinch salt
- Pinch white pepper

Directions:
1. In a food processor or blender, combine the watercress, peas, cilantro, scallions, tofu, lime juice, olives, lime zest, salt, and white pepper, and process or blend until smooth.
2. This sauce can be used immediately, or you can store it in an airtight glass container in the refrigerator up to four days.

Nutrition Info:

- Info Per Serving: Calories: 27 ; Fat: 1 g ;Saturated fat: 0 g ;Sodium: 65 mg

Simple Dijon And Honey Vinaigrette

Servings: ⅓
Cooking Time: X
Ingredients:
- 3 tablespoons olive oil
- 1½ tablespoons apple cider vinegar
- 1 tablespoon honey
- 2 teaspoons Dijon mustard
- Freshly ground black pepper

Directions:
1. In a small bowl, whisk together the oil, vinegar, honey, and mustard until emulsified.
2. Season with pepper and serve.

Nutrition Info:
- Info Per Serving: Calories: 145 ; Fat: 14 g ;Saturated fat: 2 g ;Sodium: 38 mg

Spinach And Walnut Pesto

Servings: 5
Cooking Time: X
Ingredients:
- 2 cups spinach
- ½ cup chopped walnuts
- ½ cup olive oil
- 2 tablespoons minced garlic
- ½ teaspoon salt

Directions:
1. In a blender, place the spinach, walnuts, olive oil, garlic, and salt and blend until smooth. Use immediately.

Nutrition Info:
- Info Per Serving: Calories: 275 ; Fat: 29 g ;Saturated fat: 4g ;Sodium: 243 mg

Avocado Dressing

Servings: 8
Cooking Time: 15 Minutes
Ingredients:
- 1 avocado, peeled and cubed
- ⅔ cup plain nonfat Greek yogurt
- ¼ cup buttermilk
- 2 tablespoons fresh lemon juice
- 1 tablespoon honey
- Pinch salt
- 2 tablespoons chopped fresh chives
- ½ cup chopped cherry tomatoes

Directions:
1. In a blender or food processor, combine the avocado, yogurt, buttermilk, lemon juice, honey, salt, and chives, and blend or process until smooth. Stir in the tomatoes.
2. You may need to add more buttermilk or lemon juice to achieve a pourable consistency.
3. This dressing can be stored by putting it into a small dish, then pouring about 2 teaspoons lemon juice on top. Cover the dressing by pressing plastic wrap directly onto the surface. Refrigerate for up to 1 day.

Nutrition Info:
- Info Per Serving: Calories:55 ; Fat: 3g ;Saturated fat: 1g ;Sodium: 30mg

Sun-dried Tomato And Kalamata Olive Tapenade

Servings: 1¼
Cooking Time: X
Ingredients:
- ½ cup chopped sun-dried tomatoes
- ½ cup packed fresh basil leaves
- ¼ cup sliced Kalamata olives
- ¼ cup Parmesan cheese
- 2 garlic cloves
- 1 tablespoon olive oil
- Sea salt
- Freshly ground black pepper

Directions:
1. In a food processor or blender, place the sun-dried tomatoes, basil, olives, Parmesan cheese, garlic, and olive oil and pulse until smooth.
2. Season with salt and pepper.

Nutrition Info:
- Info Per Serving: Calories: 57 ; Fat: 3 g ;Saturated fat: 1 g ;Sodium: 207 mg

Smoky Barbecue Rub

Servings: ½
Cooking Time: X
Ingredients:
- 2 tablespoons smoked paprika
- 2 tablespoons brown sugar
- 1 tablespoon chili powder
- 1 tablespoon garlic powder
- 2 teaspoons onion powder
- 2 teaspoons celery salt
- 1 teaspoon ground cumin
- ½ teaspoon sea salt
- ½ teaspoon dried oregano

Directions:
1. In a small bowl, whisk together the paprika, sugar, chili powder, garlic powder, onion powder, celery salt, cumin, salt, and oregano until well blended.
2. Transfer to an airtight container to store.

Nutrition Info:
- Info Per Serving: Calories: 23 ; Fat: 1 g ;Saturated fat: 0 g ;Sodium: 113 mg

Chimichurri Rub

Servings: ½
Cooking Time: X
Ingredients:
- 2 tablespoons dried parsley
- 2 tablespoons dried basil
- 1 tablespoon hot paprika
- 1 tablespoon dried oregano
- 2 teaspoons garlic powder
- 1 teaspoon dried thyme
- 1 teaspoon onion powder
- ½ teaspoon freshly ground black pepper
- ¼ teaspoon sea salt
- Pinch red pepper flakes

Directions:
1. In a small bowl, whisk together the parsley, basil, paprika, oregano, garlic powder, thyme, onion powder, pepper, salt, and red pepper flakes until well blended.
2. Transfer to an airtight container to store.

Nutrition Info:
- Info Per Serving: Calories: 18 ; Fat: 0 g ;Saturated fat: 0 g ;Sodium: 90 mg

Buttermilk-herb Dressing

Servings: ¾
Cooking Time: X
Ingredients:

- ½ cup buttermilk
- ¼ cup silken tofu
- 2 tablespoons minced scallion, white part only
- 1 tablespoon chopped fresh parsley
- 1 tablespoon chopped fresh thyme
- 1 teaspoon chopped fresh dill
- Sea salt
- Freshly ground black pepper

Directions:

1. In a medium bowl, whisk together the buttermilk, tofu, scallions, parsley, thyme, and dill until well blended.
2. Season with salt and pepper.

Nutrition Info:

- Info Per Serving: Calories: 17 ; Fat: 0 g ;Saturated fat: 0 g ;Sodium: 35 mg

Classic Italian Tomato Sauce

Servings: 4
Cooking Time: 20 Minutes
Ingredients:

- 2 teaspoons olive oil
- 1 onion, chopped
- 3 cloves garlic, minced
- 1½ pounds plum (Roma) tomatoes, chopped
- 2 tablespoons no-salt-added tomato paste
- 2 tablespoons finely grated carrot
- 1 teaspoon dried basil leaves
- ½ teaspoon dried oregano
- ⅛ teaspoon white pepper
- Pinch salt
- Pinch sugar
- 2 tablespoons fresh basil leaves, chopped

Directions:

1. In a large saucepan, heat the olive oil over medium heat.
2. Add the onion and garlic, and cook and stir for 3 minutes or until the onions are translucent.
3. Add the tomatoes, tomato paste, carrot, basil, oregano, white pepper, salt, and sugar, and stir and bring to a simmer.
4. Simmer for 15 to 18 minutes, stirring frequently, or until the sauce thickens slightly.
5. Stir in the fresh basil and serve.

Nutrition Info:

- Info Per Serving: Calories: 73 ; Fat: 3 g ;Saturated fat: 0 g ;Sodium: 19 mg

Lemon-garlic Sauce

Servings: 5
Cooking Time: X
Ingredients:

- ¼ cup freshly squeezed lemon juice
- 2 tablespoons olive oil
- 1 tablespoon minced garlic
- 1 tablespoon dried oregano
- ½ teaspoon salt

Directions:

1. In a small bowl, mix the lemon juice, olive oil, garlic, oregano, and salt until well blended. Use immediately.

Nutrition Info:

- Info Per Serving: Calories: 55 ; Fat: 5 g ;Saturated fat: 1 g ;Sodium: 233 mg

Sweet Potato And Navy Bean Hummus

Servings: X
Cooking Time: X
Ingredients:

- 1 cup mashed cooked sweet potato
- 1 cup low-sodium canned navy beans, rinsed and drained
- 2 tablespoons tahini
- 2 tablespoons olive oil
- Juice of 1 lime
- ½ teaspoon minced garlic
- ¼ teaspoon ground cumin
- Sea salt
- Chopped fresh cilantro, for garnish
- Pita bread, baked tortilla crisps, or veggies, for serving

Directions:
1. In a food processor or blender, add the sweet potato, beans, tahini, olive oil, lime juice, garlic, and cumin and purée until very smooth, scraping down the sides at least once.
2. Season with salt, top with cilantro, and serve with pita bread, baked tortilla crisps, or veggies.

Nutrition Info:
- Info Per Serving: Calories: 396 ; Fat: 23 g ;Saturated fat: 3 g ;Sodium: 78 mg

Mango, Peach, And Tomato Pico De Gallo

Servings: 4
Cooking Time: 15 Minutes
Ingredients:

- 1 mango, peeled and cubed (see Ingredient Tip)
- 1 peach, peeled and chopped (see Ingredient Tip)
- 1 beefsteak tomato, cored and chopped
- 1 cup yellow or red cherry tomatoes, chopped
- 2 scallions, chopped
- 1 jalapeño pepper, seeded and minced
- 2 tablespoons fresh lemon juice
- 1 teaspoon fresh grated lemon zest
- Pinch salt
- ⅛ teaspoon red pepper flakes

Directions:
1. In a medium bowl, combine the mango, peach, tomato, scallions, jalapeño pepper, lemon juice, lemon zest, salt, and red pepper flakes, and mix well.
2. Serve immediately or store in an airtight glass container in the refrigerator for up to 2 days.

Nutrition Info:
- Info Per Serving: Calories: 80 ; Fat: 1 g ;Saturated fat: 0 g ;Sodium: 48 mg

Tasty Tomato Sauce

Servings: 5
Cooking Time: 5 Minutes
Ingredients:

- 6 tablespoons low-sodium ketchup
- 2 tablespoons minced garlic
- 1½ tablespoons honey
- 1 tablespoon vinegar
- ½ teaspoon freshly ground black pepper

Directions:
1. In a small bowl, mix the ketchup, garlic, honey, vinegar, and pepper until well blended. Use immediately.

Nutrition Info:
- Info Per Serving: Calories: 46 ; Fat: 0g ;Saturated fat: 0g ;Sodium: 5 mg

Spicy Peanut Sauce

Servings: 8
Cooking Time: 15 Minutes
Ingredients:
- ½ cup powdered peanut butter (see Ingredient Tip)
- 2 tablespoons reduced-fat peanut butter
- ⅓ cup plain nonfat Greek yogurt
- 2 tablespoons fresh lime juice
- 2 teaspoons low-sodium soy sauce
- 1 scallion, chopped
- 1 clove garlic, minced
- 1 jalapeño pepper, seeded and minced
- ⅛ teaspoon red pepper flakes

Directions:
1. In a blender or food processor, combine powdered peanut butter, reduced-fat peanut butter, yogurt, lime juice, soy sauce, scallion, garlic, jalapeño pepper, and red pepper flakes, and blend or process until smooth.
2. Serve immediately or store in an airtight glass container and refrigerate for up to 3 days. You can thin this sauce with more lime juice if necessary.

Nutrition Info:
- Info Per Serving: Calories: 60 ; Fat: 3 g ;Saturated fat: 0 g ;Sodium: 88 mg

Silken Fruited Tofu Cream

Servings: 4
Cooking Time: 15 Minutes
Ingredients:
- 1 cup silken tofu
- ⅓ cup fresh raspberries
- 2 tablespoons orange-pineapple juice
- 1 tablespoon fresh lemon juice
- ½ teaspoon vanilla extract
- ⅛ teaspoon ground cinnamon
- Pinch salt

Directions:
1. In a blender or food processor, combine the tofu, raspberries, orange-pineapple juice, lemon juice, vanilla, cinnamon, and salt. Blend or process until smooth.
2. You can use this cream immediately or store it in an airtight glass container in the refrigerator for up to 2 days.

Nutrition Info:
- Info Per Serving: Calories: 49 ; Fat: 2 g ;Saturated fat: 0 g ;Sodium: 23 mg

Sweet Salad Dressing

Servings: 5
Cooking Time: X
Ingredients:

- ¼ cup low-sodium Worcestershire sauce (or ¼ cup Worcestershire sauce)
- 2 tablespoons minced garlic
- 1½ tablespoons honey
- 2 teaspoons onion powder
- ½ teaspoon freshly ground black pepper

Directions:

1. In a small bowl, mix the Worcestershire sauce, garlic, honey, onion powder, and pepper until well blended. Use immediately.

Nutrition Info:

- Info Per Serving: Calories: 39 ; Fat: 0g ;Saturated fat: 0g ;Sodium: 136mg

Zesty Citrus Kefir Dressing

Servings: 8
Cooking Time: 15 Minutes
Ingredients:

- ⅔ cup kefir
- 2 tablespoons honey
- 2 tablespoons low-sodium yellow mustard
- 2 tablespoons fresh lemon juice
- ½ teaspoon fresh lemon zest
- 1 tablespoon fresh orange juice
- ½ teaspoon fresh orange zest
- 1 teaspoon olive oil
- Pinch salt

Directions:

1. In a blender or food processor, combine the kefir, honey, mustard, lemon juice and zest, orange juice and zest, olive oil, and salt. Blend or process until smooth.
2. You can serve this dressing immediately, or store it in an airtight container in the refrigerator for up to 3 days.

Nutrition Info:

- Info Per Serving: Calories: 37 ; Fat: 1 g ;Saturated fat: 0 g ;Sodium: 43 mg

Desserts And Treats

Chocolate Chia Pudding

Servings: 2
Cooking Time: 4 Hours
Ingredients:
- 1 cup low-fat milk
- ½ cup chia seeds
- 2 tablespoons cocoa powder
- 1 tablespoon maple syrup
- 1 tablespoon vanilla extract

Directions:
1. In a small bowl, combine the milk, chia seeds, cocoa powder, maple syrup, and vanilla extract.
2. Let the mixture stand for 10 to 15 minutes, stir again, and divide it between 2 Mason jars or lidded containers. Seal and refrigerate for 4 hours or overnight.

Nutrition Info:
- Info Per Serving: Calories:383 ; Fat: 19g ;Saturated fat: 3g ;Sodium: 66mg

Almond Cheesecake–stuffed Apples

Servings: X
Cooking Time: 25 Minutes
Ingredients:
- 2 small apples, cut in half and cores scooped out on each side
- 1 teaspoon canola oil
- 2 tablespoons brown sugar, divided
- ⅛ teaspoon ground cinnamon
- ¼ cup fat-free cream cheese
- ⅛ teaspoon almond extract
- 2 tablespoons chopped almonds, for garnish

Directions:
1. Preheat the oven to 400°F.
2. Line a small baking dish with parchment paper and arrange the apple halves in the dish, cut-side up.
3. Brush the cut side of the apples with the canola oil. Sprinkle 1 tablespoon brown sugar and the cinnamon over the halves.
4. Place in the oven and bake for 15 minutes.
5. While the apples are baking, in a small bowl, stir together the cream cheese, remaining 1 tablespoon brown sugar, and almond extract until well blended.
6. Evenly divide the cream cheese mixture among the apple halves and bake for 10 more minutes.
7. Top with almonds and serve.

Nutrition Info:
- Info Per Serving: Calories: 307 ; Fat: 16 g ;Saturated fat: 7 g ;Sodium: 90 mg

Loco Pie Crust

Servings: 8
Cooking Time: X
Ingredients:
- ½ cup plus
- 1 tablespoon mayonnaise
- 3 tablespoons buttermilk
- 1 teaspoon vinegar
- 1½ cups flour

Directions:
1. In large bowl, combine mayonnaise, buttermilk, and vinegar and mix well. Add flour, stirring with a fork to form a ball. You may need to add more buttermilk or more flour to make a workable dough. Press dough into a ball, wrap in plastic wrap, and refrigerate for 1 hour.
2. When ready to bake, preheat oven to 400ºF. Roll out dough between two sheets of waxed paper. Remove top sheet and place crust in 9″ pie pan. Carefully ease off the top sheet of paper, then ease the crust into the pan and press to bottom and sides. Fold edges under and flute.
3. Either use as recipe directs, or bake for 5 minutes, then press crust down with fork if necessary. Bake for 5–8 minutes longer or until crust is light golden brown.

Nutrition Info:
- Info Per Serving: Calories:171.83; Fat: 7.35 g ;Saturated fat:1.18 g;Sodium: 65.46 mg

Banana-rum Mousse

Servings: 4
Cooking Time: X
Ingredients:
- 3 tablespoons rum
- 2 tablespoons lime juice
- 2 tablespoons powdered sugar
- 2 bananas, chopped
- 1 cup vanilla frozen yogurt
- 4 sprigs fresh mint

Directions:
1. In blender or food processor, combine the rum, lime juice, sugar, and bananas and blend or process until smooth.
2. Add the yogurt and blend or process until smooth, scraping down sides once during blending. Spoon into dessert glasses and serve immediately, or cover and freeze up to 8 hours before serving.

Nutrition Info:
- Info Per Serving: Calories:164.58 ; Fat: 2.25 g ;Saturated fat: 1.13 g;Sodium:32.30 mg

Cashew Butter Latte

Servings: 1
Cooking Time: 10 Min
Ingredients:
- ¼ cup unsalted cashew butter
- 1 tsp vanilla extract
- 1 tsp organic honey
- ½ tsp ground cinnamon, plus more if needed
- 1 cup unsweetened cashew milk, more if needed

Directions:
1. Add the espresso, cashew butter, vanilla extract, honey, and cinnamon into a medium-sized stockpot over medium heat, whisking occasionally until the cashew butter has melted.
2. Heat the cashew milk over low heat in a small-sized stockpot. When it is warm (not hot), whisk it vigorously by hand, or use a handheld beater, to make it foamy.
3. Pour the hot coffee mixture into a mug and top with the foamy milk.

Nutrition Info:
- Info Per Serving: Calories: 169 ; Fat: 3 g ;Saturated fat:2 g ;Sodium: 128 mg

Mango Blood Orange Sorbet

Servings: 4
Cooking Time: 5 Minutes
Ingredients:
- 2 cups frozen mango cubes
- 2 tablespoons lemon juice
- ⅓ cup blood orange juice (see Ingredient Tip)
- 3 tablespoons sugar

Directions:
1. In a high-speed blender or food processor, combine the mango, lemon juice, blood orange juice, and sugar, and process until smooth.
2. Serve immediately, or freeze for a denser texture.

Nutrition Info:
- Info Per Serving: Calories:100 ; Fat: 0g ;Saturated fat: 0g ;Sodium: 2 mg

Chocolate, Peanut Butter, And Banana Ice Cream

Servings: 2
Cooking Time: X
Ingredients:
- 2 frozen bananas, peeled and sliced
- 2 tablespoons cocoa powder
- 1 tablespoon honey
- 2 tablespoons all-natural peanut butter
- 1 tablespoon chopped walnuts (or nut of choice)

Directions:
1. Put the frozen bananas, cocoa powder, honey, and peanut butter into a high-speed blender and blend until smooth.
2. Transfer the ice cream mixture into a resealable container and freeze for 2 hours.
3. Once frozen, scoop the ice cream into two serving bowls and top with walnuts.

Nutrition Info:
- Info Per Serving: Calories: 269 ; Fat: 12 g ;Saturated fat: 2 g ;Sodium: 5 mg

Maple-walnut Pots De Crème

Servings: X
Cooking Time: 5 Minutes
Ingredients:
- ½ cup unsweetened soy milk
- ¼ teaspoon pure vanilla extract
- 1½ teaspoons unflavored gelatin
- ½ cup fat-free vanilla Greek yogurt
- ½ cup low-fat buttermilk
- ⅓ cup maple syrup
- Pinch sea salt
- 2 tablespoons chopped walnuts, for garnish

Directions:
1. In a small saucepan, stir together the soy milk and vanilla over medium heat until just warmer than room temperature, about 2 minutes.
2. Stir in the gelatin and heat the mixture until scalded, but not boiling, about 3 minutes.
3. Remove the saucepan from the heat and set aside to cool for 10 minutes.
4. Whisk in the yogurt, buttermilk, maple syrup, and salt until well blended.
5. Pour the mixture into 2 (6-ounce) ramekins and chill, covered, in the refrigerator until completely set, at least 4 hours.
6. Serve topped with walnuts.

Nutrition Info:
- Info Per Serving: Calories: 301; Fat: 6g ;Saturated fat: 1g ;Sodium: 200 mg

Crepes With Poached Pears

Servings: 6
Cooking Time: X
Ingredients:

- 1 egg 1 egg white
- ½ cup 1% milk
- ½ cup flour
- 2 tablespoons sugar
- 2 tablespoons melted butter, divided
- 4 pears
- ¼ cup sugar
- 2 tablespoons lemon juice
- ¼ cup pear nectar
- ½ cup frozen non-dairy whipped topping, thawed
- 1 cup fresh raspberries
- 2 tablespoons powdered sugar

Directions:
1. In blender or food processor, combine egg, egg whites, milk, flour, sugar, and 1 tablespoon melted butter, and blend or process until smooth. Let stand for 15 minutes.
2. Heat a 7″ nonstick skillet over medium heat. Brush with 1 tablespoon melted butter. Using a ¼-cup measure, pour 3 tablespoons batter into the skillet; immediately rotate and tilt skillet to spread batter evenly. Cook over medium heat for 1–2 minutes or until the crepe can be moved.
3. Loosen the edges of the crepe and flip; cook for 1 minute on second side, then turn out onto kitchen towels. Stack between layers of waxed or parchment paper when cool.
4. For filling, peel and chop pears and place in medium saucepan with sugar and lemon juice. Pour pear nectar over. Bring to a simmer over medium-high heat, then cook, stirring gently, until pears are very tender, about 3–5 minutes.
5. Let pears cool in liquid. When ready to serve, fold pear mixture into whipped topping. Fill crepes with this mixture and place, seam side down, on serving plates. Garnish with raspberries and sprinkle with powdered sugar.

Nutrition Info:
- Info Per Serving: Calories: 185.51; Fat:5.93 g ;Saturated fat:3.54 g;Sodium:62.39 mg

Double Chocolate Cinnamon Nice Cream

Servings: 4
Cooking Time: 5 Minutes
Ingredients:

- 3 tablespoons semisweet chocolate chips
- 2 frozen bananas, cut into chunks
- ⅓ cup frozen mango cubes
- 2 Medjool dates, pit removed and chopped (see Ingredient Tip)
- 2 tablespoons flax or soy milk
- 3 tablespoons cocoa powder
- ½ teaspoon vanilla extract
- ½ teaspoon ground cinnamon
- Pinch salt

Directions:
1. In a small saucepan over low heat, melt the semisweet chocolate chips, stirring frequently. Transfer the melted chocolate from the pan to a small bowl to cool, and place it in the refrigerator while you prepare the rest of the ingredients. (Make sure to not let the chocolate harden.)
2. In a blender or food processor, combine the bananas, mangoes, dates, and milk and blend until well combined.
3. Add the cocoa powder, vanilla, cinnamon, salt, and the melted, cooled chocolate. Blend until the mixture is smooth.
4. This treat can be served right away or frozen for 2 to 3 hours before serving.

Nutrition Info:
- Info Per Serving: Calories: 221 ; Fat: 5 g ;Saturated fat: 4 g ;Sodium: 8 mg

Peach Melba Frozen Yogurt Parfaits

Servings: 4
Cooking Time: 5 Minutes
Ingredients:
- 2 tablespoons slivered almonds
- 1 tablespoon brown sugar
- 2 peaches, peeled and chopped (see Ingredient Tip)
- 1 cup fresh raspberries
- 2 cups no-sugar-added vanilla frozen yogurt
- 2 tablespoons peach jam
- 2 tablespoons raspberry jam or preserves

Directions:
1. In a small nonstick skillet over medium heat, combine the almonds and brown sugar.
2. Cook, stirring frequently, until the sugar melts and coats the almonds, about 3 to 4 minutes. Remove from the heat and put the almonds on a plate to cool.
3. To make the parfaits: In four parfait or wine glasses, layer each with the peaches, raspberries, frozen yogurt, peach jam, and raspberry jam. Top each glass with the caramelized almonds.

Nutrition Info:
- Info Per Serving: Calories: 263 ; Fat: 5 g ;Saturated fat: 1 g ;Sodium: 91 mg

Blueberry-hazelnut Crisp

Servings: 8
Cooking Time: X
Ingredients:
- 3 cups blueberries
- ¼ cup sugar
- 1 teaspoon cinnamon
- ½ teaspoon nutmeg
- 1½ cups quick-cooking oatmeal
- ½ cup flour
- ¼ cup whole-wheat flour
- ½ cup brown sugar
- ½ cup chopped hazelnuts
- 1/3 cup butter or margarine, melted

Directions:
1. Preheat oven to 350°F. Spray a 9″ round cake pan with nonstick cooking spray and set aside.
2. Combine blueberries in medium bowl with sugar, cinnamon, and nutmeg. Spoon into prepared pan.
3. In same bowl, combine oatmeal, flour, whole-wheat flour, brown sugar, and hazelnuts and mix well. Add melted butter and mix until crumbly. Sprinkle over fruit in dish.
4. Bake for 35–45 minutes or until fruit bubbles and topping is browned and crisp. Let cool for 15 minutes before serving.

Nutrition Info:
- Info Per Serving: Calories:373.56; Fat:14.57 g ;Saturated fat: 5.59 g;Sodium: 61.35 mg

Choc Chip Banana Muffins

Servings: 8
Cooking Time: 20 Min
Ingredients:
- 2 tbsp. ground flaxseeds
- 5 tbsp. water
- 2 cups almond flour
- 1 tbsp. ground cinnamon
- 1 tsp baking powder
- 3 (1 cup) medium ripe bananas, mashed
- 2 tbsp. organic honey
- ¼ cup dark chocolate chips
- 1 tsp vanilla extract
- ¼ cup unsalted walnuts, chopped

Directions:
1. Heat the oven to 375°F gas mark 5. Line a muffin tin with 8 muffin cup liners. Set aside.
2. In a small-sized mixing bowl, stir in the flaxseeds and water and let this sit for 5 minutes until the mixture congeals.
3. In a large-sized mixing bowl, add the almond flour, cinnamon, and baking powder and mix to combine.
4. In a medium-sized mixing bowl, add the flaxseed mixture, bananas, honey, chocolate chips, and vanilla extract, mix to combine. Slowly pour the wet ingredients into the dry ingredients, mix well. Add in the walnuts and mix.
5. Spoon the mixture evenly into the 8 lined muffin tin, bake for 20 minutes, or until the inserted toothpick comes out clean.
6. Serve warm or once completely cooled, store in an airtight container to stay fresh.

Nutrition Info:
- Info Per Serving: Calories: 199 ; Fat: 5 g ;Saturated fat: 1 g ;Sodium: 64 mg

Apple Pear-nut Crisp

Servings: 8
Cooking Time: X
Ingredients:
- 2 apples, sliced
- 3 pears, sliced
- 2 tablespoons lemon juice
- ¼ cup sugar
- 1 teaspoon cinnamon
- ½ teaspoon nutmeg
- 1½ cups quick-cooking oatmeal
- ½ cup flour
- ¼ cup whole-wheat flour
- ½ cup brown sugar
- 1/3 cup butter or margarine, melted

Directions:
1. Preheat oven to 350ºF. Spray a 9″ round cake pan with nonstick cooking spray and set aside.
2. Prepare apples and pears, sprinkling with lemon juice as you work. Combine in medium bowl with sugar, cinnamon, and nutmeg. Spoon into prepared cake pan.
3. In same bowl, combine oatmeal, flour, whole-wheat flour, and brown sugar and mix well. Add melted butter and mix until crumbly. Sprinkle over fruit in dish.
4. Bake for 35–45 minutes or until fruit bubbles and topping is browned and crisp. Let cool for 15 minutes before serving.

Nutrition Info:
- Info Per Serving: Calories: 353.77; Fat:9.97 g ;Saturated fat: 5.25 g;Sodium: 61.78 mg

Curried Fruit Compote

Servings: 6
Cooking Time: 10 Minutes
Ingredients:
- 1 (8-ounce) can pineapple chunks, undrained
- 1 ripe pear, peeled and chopped
- 1 Granny Smith apple, chopped
- ⅓ cup dried cranberries
- 1 cup apple juice
- 1 tablespoon fresh lemon juice
- 2 tablespoons agave nectar or packed brown sugar
- 1 tablespoon curry powder
- 1 tablespoon cornstarch
- Pinch salt

Directions:
1. In a medium saucepan over medium heat, combine the pineapple chunks, pear, apple, cranberries, apple juice, lemon juice, agave nectar (or brown sugar), curry powder, cornstarch, and salt. Stir to blend.
2. Bring to a boil, reduce the heat to low, and simmer for 6 to 8 minutes or until the fruit is tender.
3. At this point, you can serve the compote as-is, or you can purée all—or part—of it. The compote can be stored in the refrigerator for up to 3 days. You can rewarm the compote on the stovetop before you serve it.

Nutrition Info:
- Info Per Serving: Calories: 112 ; Fat: 0 g ;Saturated fat: 0 g ;Sodium: 4 mg

Oatmeal Brownies

Servings: 16
Cooking Time: X
Ingredients:
- ¼ cup prune puree
- ¼ cup finely chopped dates
- ½ cup all-purpose flour
- ½ cup ground oatmeal
- ½ cup cocoa powder
- ½ teaspoon baking soda
- ½ cup brown sugar
- ¼ cup sugar
- 1 egg
- 1 egg white
- ¼ cup chocolate yogurt
- 2 teaspoons vanilla
- 2 tablespoons butter or plant sterol margarine, melted
- ½ cup dark-chocolate chips

Directions:
1. Preheat oven to 350ºF. Spray an 8″ square baking pan with nonstick cooking spray containing flour and set aside.
2. In small bowl, combine prune puree and dates; mix well and set aside. In large bowl, combine flour, oatmeal, cocoa, baking soda, brown sugar, and sugar, and mix well.
3. Add egg, egg white, yogurt, vanilla, and butter to prune mixture and mix well. Add to flour mixture and stir just until blended. Spoon into prepared pan and smooth top. Bake for 22–30 minutes or until edges are set but the center is still slightly soft. Remove from oven and place on wire rack.
4. In microwave-safe bowl, place chocolate chips. Microwave on 50 percent power for 1 minute, then remove and stir. Microwave for 30 seconds longer, then stir. If necessary, repeat microwave process until chips are melted. Pour over warm brownies and gently spread to cover. Let cool completely and cut into bars.

Nutrition Info:
- Info Per Serving: Calories:153.83; Fat: 4.88 g ;Saturated fat:2.63 g;Sodium:63.58 mg

Whole-wheat Chocolate Chip Cookies

Servings: 48
Cooking Time: X

Ingredients:

- ¼ cup butter or plant sterol margarine, softened
- 1½ cups brown sugar
- ½ cup applesauce
- 1 tablespoon vanilla
- 1 egg
- 2 egg whites
- 2½ cups whole-wheat pastry flour
- ½ cup ground oatmeal
- 1 teaspoon baking soda
- ¼ teaspoon salt
- 2 cups special dark chocolate chips
- 1 cup chopped hazelnuts

Directions:

1. Preheat oven to 375ºF. Line cookie sheets with parchment paper or Sil-pat silicone liners and set aside.
2. In large bowl, combine butter, brown sugar, and applesauce and beat well until smooth. Add vanilla, egg, and egg whites and beat until combined.
3. Add flour, oatmeal, baking soda, and salt and mix until a dough forms. Fold in chocolate chips and hazelnuts.
4. Drop dough by rounded teaspoons onto prepared cookie sheets. Bake for 7–10 minutes or until cookies are light golden brown and set. Let cool for 5 minutes before removing from cookie sheet to wire rack to cool.

Nutrition Info:

- Info Per Serving: Calories: 114.86; Fat:4.89 g ;Saturated fat:2.04 g;Sodium:26.49 mg

Silken Chocolate Mousse

Servings: 6
Cooking Time: X

Ingredients:

- 2 (1-ounce) squares unsweetened chocolate
- 2 tablespoons butter
- ½ cup sugar
- 1 teaspoon vanilla
- ½ cup satin or silken soft tofu
- 1 cup chocolate frozen yogurt
- 1 cup frozen non-dairy whipped topping, thawed

Directions:

1. Chop chocolate and place in small microwave-safe bowl with the butter. Microwave on medium for 2–4 minutes, stirring twice during cooking time, until chocolate is melted and mixture is smooth. Stir in sugar until sugar dissolves.
2. In blender or food processor, place chocolate mixture and add vanilla and tofu. Blend or process until smooth. If necessary, let cool for 10–15 minutes or until lukewarm.
3. Then add the frozen yogurt and blend or process until smooth. Finally add the whipped topping and blend or process until just mixed. Spoon into serving glasses, cover, and chill for 4–6 hours before serving.

Nutrition Info:

- Info Per Serving: Calories: 219.73; Fat:12.12 g ;Saturated fat: 7.86 g;Sodium:78.14 mg

Strawberry-rhubarb Parfait

Servings: 6
Cooking Time: X
Ingredients:

- 2 stalks rhubarb, sliced
- ½ cup apple juice
- 1/3 cup sugar
- 1 (10-ounce) package frozen strawberries
- 3 cups frozen vanilla yogurt

Directions:

1. In medium saucepan, combine rhubarb, apple juice, and sugar. Bring to a simmer, then reduce heat and simmer for 8–10 minutes or until rhubarb is soft.
2. Remove pan from heat and immediately stir in frozen strawberries, stirring to break up strawberries. Let stand until cool, about 30 minutes.
3. Layer rhubarb mixture and frozen yogurt in parfait glasses or goblets, starting and ending with rhubarb mixture. Cover and freeze until firm, about 8 hours.

Nutrition Info:

- Info Per Serving: Calories:210.56; Fat: 4.16 g ;Saturated fat: 2.48 g;Sodium: 64.41 mg

Apple Cheesecake

Servings: 2
Cooking Time: 25 Min
Ingredients:

- Aluminum foil
- 2 small honey crisp apples, cut in half and core removed
- 1 tsp coconut oil, melted
- 2 tbsp. organic honey, divided
- ⅛ tsp ground cinnamon
- ¼ cup fat-free cream cheese
- ⅛ tsp vanilla extract
- 2 tbsp. walnuts, chopped for garnish

Directions:

1. Heat the oven to 400°F gas mark 6.
2. Line a baking sheet with aluminum foil and arrange the apple halves on the sheet, cut side up.
3. Brush the cut side of the apples with coconut oil. Drizzle 1 tbsp. honey and sprinkle the cinnamon over the apple halves. Bake for 15 minutes.
4. While the apples are baking, in a small-sized mixing bowl, add the cream cheese, remaining 1 tbsp. organic honey, and vanilla extract, mix until well blended.
5. Divide the cream cheese mixture among the apple halves and bake for 10 minutes.
6. Garnish with walnuts and serve.

Nutrition Info:

- Info Per Serving: Calories: 307 ; Fat: 16g;Saturated fat: 7 g ;Sodium: 90 mg

Almond Strawberry Parfaits

Servings: 4
Cooking Time: 5 Minutes
Ingredients:

- ¼ cup sliced almonds
- ½ cup low-fat ricotta cheese
- ½ cup plain nonfat Greek yogurt
- 3 tablespoons powdered sugar
- ½ teaspoon vanilla
- Pinch salt
- 2 cups sliced strawberries
- 2 tablespoons strawberry jam
- 1 tablespoon balsamic vinegar

Directions:

1. In a small saucepan on the stovetop or in a glass bowl in the toaster oven, toast the almonds over low heat until they are golden. Transfer to a plate and set aside.
2. In a small bowl, combine the ricotta, yogurt, powdered sugar, vanilla, and salt.
3. In a medium bowl, combine the sliced strawberries, jam, and balsamic vinegar, and mix gently.
4. Make the parfaits by layering the ricotta mixture and the strawberry mixture into 4 parfait or wine glasses. Top each glass with the toasted almonds, and serve. You can make this recipe ahead of time and chill it up to 3 hours.

Nutrition Info:

- Info Per Serving: Calories: 158 ; Fat: 6 g ;Saturated fat: 2 g ;Sodium: 62 mg

Dark Chocolate Brownie Bites

Servings: 12
Cooking Time: 18 Minutes
Ingredients:

- ¼ cup salted butter, melted
- ¼ cup puréed beets
- ½ cup packed brown sugar
- 3 tablespoons honey
- 1 teaspoon vanilla extract
- 1 egg
- 1 egg white
- Pinch salt
- ¼ teaspoon baking powder
- ½ cup whole-wheat flour
- ¼ cup all-purpose flour
- ⅓ cup cocoa powder

Directions:

1. Preheat the oven to 350°F. Line 24 mini muffin cups with mini paper liners and set aside.
2. In a medium bowl, combine the butter, beets, brown sugar, honey, and vanilla and mix well.
3. Add the egg and the egg white and beat until smooth.
4. In a separate medium bowl, combine the salt, baking powder, whole-wheat flour, all-purpose flour, and cocoa powder. Stir the dry ingredients into the butter-sugar mixture just until combined.
5. Spoon the batter among the prepared muffin cups, filling each about ⅔ full. Each cup should take about 1 tablespoon of batter.
6. Bake for 16 to 18 minutes or until the little brownies are set; they will have a shiny crust. A toothpick inserted into the center will come out with moist crumbs attached. Don't overbake them or they will be hard.
7. Let the brownie bites cool for 5 minutes, then remove them to a cooling rack. You can eat these warm or cool. Store in an airtight container at room temperature up to 3 days.

Nutrition Info:

- Info Per Serving: Calories: 141 ; Fat: 5 g ;Saturated fat: 2 g ;Sodium: 51 mg

30 day meal plan

Day 1
Breakfast: Cinnamon-hazelnut Scones
Lunch: Creamed Rice
Dinner: Crunchy Chicken Coleslaw Salad

Day 2
Breakfast: Basil-tomato Pizza
Lunch: Balsamic Blueberry Chicken
Dinner: Hearty Vegetable Stew

Day 3
Breakfast: Tofu And Cucumber Spring Rolls
Lunch: Chicken Paillards With Mushrooms
Dinner: Baba Ghanoush With Fennel Stew

Day 4
Breakfast: Lean Beef Lettuce Wraps
Lunch: Piña Colada Chicken
Dinner: Cannellini Bean–stuffed Sweet Potatoes

Day 5
Breakfast: Rolled Oats Cereal
Lunch: Chicken Stir-fry With Napa Cabbage
Dinner: Southwestern Millet-stuffed Tomatoes

Day 6
Breakfast: Cranberry Orange Mixed Grain Granola
Lunch: Lime Chicken Wraps
Dinner: Broccoli Stuffed Sweetato

Day 7
Breakfast: Cranberry-orange Bread
Lunch: Nutty Coconut Chicken With Fruit Sauce
Dinner: Bean And Veggie Cassoulet

Day 8
Breakfast: Steel-cut Oatmeal With Dried Apples And Pecans
Lunch: Tandoori Turkey Pizzas
Dinner:

Day 9
Breakfast: Savory Breakfast Rice Porridge
Lunch: Chicken Rice
Dinner: Butter Bean Rotini

Day 10
Breakfast: Cranberry Hotcakes
Lunch: Lemon Tarragon Turkey Medallions
Dinner: Risotto With Artichokes

Day 11
Breakfast: Panzanella Breakfast Casserole
Lunch: Turkey Curry With Fruit
Dinner: Chopped Vegetable Tabbouleh

Day 12
Breakfast: Raisin Breakfast Cookies
Lunch: Grilled Turkey And Veggie Kabobs
Dinner: Potato Soufflé

Day 13
Breakfast: Dutch Apple Omelet
Lunch: Sautéed Chicken With Roasted Garlic Sauce
Dinner: Spaghetti Squash Skillet

Day 14
Breakfast: French Toast With Citrus Compote
Lunch:"butter" Chicken
Dinner: Kidney Bean Stew

Day 15
Breakfast: Fish Tacos
Lunch: Moroccan Chicken
Dinner: Quinoa Pepper Pilaf

Day 16
Breakfast: Strawberry Granola Parfaits
Lunch: Chicken Pesto
Dinner: Caramelized Spiced Carrots

Day 17
Breakfast: Strawberry Yogurt Tarts
Lunch: Turkey Cutlets Parmesan
Dinner: Asparagus With Almond Topping

Day 18
Breakfast: Curried Farro Hot Cereal
Lunch: Italian Chicken Bake
Dinner: Apple Coleslaw

Day 19
Breakfast: Dark-chocolate Orange Scones
Lunch: Lime Turkey Skewers
Dinner: Cucumber-mango Salad

Day 20
Breakfast: Crisp Polenta Open-faced Sandwiches
Lunch: Cashew Chicken
Dinner: Sesame Spinach

Day 21
Breakfast: Turkey Oat Patties
Lunch: Pork And Beef Mains
Dinner: Roasted-garlic Corn

Day 22
Breakfast: Simple Pork Burgers
Lunch: Sirloin Steak With Root Vegetables
Dinner: Fruity Rice Salad

Day 23
Breakfast: Halibut Burgers
Lunch: Pork Quesadillas
Dinner: Cabbage-tomato-bean Chowder

Day 24
Breakfast: Citrus Cod Bake
Lunch: Pork Scallops With Spinach
Dinner: Hearty Bean And Quinoa Stew

Day 25
Breakfast: Catalán Salmon Tacos
Lunch: Cowboy Steak With Chimichurri Sauce
Dinner: Butternut Squash And Lentil Soup

Day 26
Breakfast: Pinto Bean Tortillas
Lunch: Meatball Pizza
Dinner: Summer Pineapple Fruit Salad

Day 27
Breakfast: Crisp Polenta With Tomato Sauce
Lunch: Pork Bahmi Goreng
Dinner: Minestrone Florentine Soup

Day 28
Breakfast: Spanish Omelet
Lunch: Pork Goulash
Dinner: Carrot Peach Soup

Day 29
Breakfast: Butternut Squash, Bulgur, And Tempeh Burritos
Lunch: Sirloin Meatballs In Sauce
Dinner: Veggie-stuffed Tomatoes

Day 30
Breakfast: Pumpkin And Chickpea Patties
Lunch: Whole-wheat Spaghetti And Meatballs
Dinner: Speedy Chicken Alphabet Soup

INDEX

Chicken Pesto 30
Chicken Rice 26
Chicken Stir-fry With Napa Cabbage 23
Chimichurri Rub 79
Chinese Skewered Chicken 71
Choc Chip Banana Muffins 89
Chocolate Chia Pudding 84
Chocolate, Peanut Butter, And Banana Ice Cream 86
Chopped Vegetable Tabbouleh 63
Cinnamon-hazelnut Scones 12
Citrus Cod Bake 52
Classic Italian Tomato Sauce 80
Cod Satay 48
Cowboy Steak With Chimichurri Sauce 34
Cranberry Hotcakes 17
Cranberry Orange Mixed Grain Granola 14
Cranberry-orange Bread 15
Creamed Rice 15
Crepes With Poached Pears 87
Crisp Polenta Open-faced Sandwiches 21
Crisp Polenta With Tomato Sauce 61
Crunchy Chicken Coleslaw Salad 25
Cucumber-mango Salad 68
Curried Farro Hot Cereal 20
Curried Fruit Compote 90

D

Dark Beer Beef Chili 40
Dark Chocolate Brownie Bites 93
Dark-chocolate Orange Scones 21
Double Chocolate Cinnamon Nice Cream 87
Double Tomato Sauce 76
Dutch Apple Omelet 18

F

Fennel-grilled Haddock 47
Fiery Pork Stir-fry 43
Fish Tacos 19
French Toast With Citrus Compote 19
Fresh Lime Salsa 76
Fried Mahi-mahi 48
Fruity Rice Salad 69

G

H

I

K

L

M

N

Northwest Salmon 49
Nuts On The Go 73
Nutty Coconut Chicken With Fruit Sauce 24

O

Oatmeal Brownies 90
Orange Thyme Red Snapper 51

P

Panzanella Breakfast Casserole 17
Peach Melba Frozen Yogurt Parfaits 88
Peanut-butter-banana Skewered Sammies 56
Piña Colada Chicken 23
Pinto Bean Tortillas 59
Poached Chilean Sea Bass With Pears 53
Poached Fish With Tomatoes And Capers 45
Pork And Fennel Stir Fry 38
Pork Bahmi Goreng 35
Pork Chops With Cabbage 42
Pork Goulash 36
Pork Quesadillas 33
Pork Scallops With Spinach 34
Potato Soufflé 64
Pumpkin And Chickpea Patties 63

Q

Quinoa Pepper Pilaf 65

R

Raisin Breakfast Cookies 18
Red Lentil Soup 75
Risotto With Artichokes 62
Roasted Garlic 66
Roasted Garlic Soufflé 60
Roasted Shrimp And Veggies 46
Roasted-garlic Corn 68
Rolled Oats Cereal 14

S

Salmon Vegetable Stir-fry 44

Salmon With Farro Pilaf 46

Salmon With Spicy Mixed Beans 44

Sautéed Chicken With Roasted Garlic Sauce 28

Savory Breakfast Rice Porridge 16

Sesame Spinach 68

Sesame-crusted Mahi Mahi 51

Shrimp Stir-fry 52

Silken Chocolate Mousse 91

Silken Fruited Tofu Cream 82

Simple Dijon And Honey Vinaigrette 78

Simple Pork Burgers 38

Sirloin Meatballs In Sauce 36

Sirloin Steak With Root Vegetables 33

Skillet Beef Macaroni 42

Smoky Barbecue Rub 79

Smoky Bean And Lentil Chili 55

Southwestern Millet-stuffed Tomatoes 58

Spaghetti Sauce 55

Spaghetti Squash Skillet 64

Spanish Omelet 61

Speedy Chicken Alphabet Soup 74

Spicy Peanut Sauce 82

Spinach And Walnut Pesto 78

Steak-and-pepper Kabobs 39

Steel-cut Oatmeal With Dried Apples And Pecans 16

Strawberry Granola Parfaits 20

Strawberry Yogurt Tarts 20

Strawberry-rhubarb Parfait 92

Summer Pineapple Fruit Salad 71

Sun-dried Tomato And Kalamata Olive Tapenade 79

Sweet Potato And Navy Bean Hummus 81

Sweet Salad Dressing 83

T

V

W

Z

Printed in Great Britain
by Amazon

27190616R00057